Living
and Dying
in Zazen

Living and Dying in Zazen

Five Zen Masters of Modern Japan

Arthur Braverman

WEATHERHILL

Boston • London

Weatherhill
An imprint of Shambhala Publications, Inc.
2129 13th Street
Boulder, Colorado 80302
www.shambhala.com

Protected by copyright under terms of the International Copyright Union.

All rights reserved. No part of this book may be reproduced in any form or by any means, electronic or mechanical, including photocopying, recording, or by any information storage and retrieval system, without permission in writing from the publisher.

Weatherhill is distributed worldwide by Penguin Random House, Inc., and its subsidiaries.

Library of Congress Cataloging-in-Publication Data available upon request.

ISBN 978-0-83480-531-6

The authorized representative in the EU for product safety and compliance is eucomply OÜ, Pärnu mnt 139b-14, 11317 Tallinn, Estonia, hello@eucompliancepartner.com.

153046648

CONTENTS

Introduction • 7

1 Sodō Yokoyama • 11

2 Kōdō Sawaki • 50

3 Kōzan Katō • 79

4 Motoko Ikebe • 112

5 Dying in Zazen • 135

A photographic insert follows page 96

DEDICATION

To the memories of two very special monks:
Reverend Kōshi Ichida and Abbot Shinyū Miyaura

# INTRODUCTION

In 1969, I traveled to Japan in search of a place to practice Zen Buddhism under the guidance of a Zen master. I was excited to be traveling in the Far East. Many Westerners took to the road in search of alternative ways to live, having been wakened from a state of lethargy when the affluent United States led its people blindly into the Vietnam War. We were an international family bonded by our refusal to buy into a world whose values we didn't share.

Like so many who chose to explore Zen Buddhism as part of an alternative lifestyle, my head was already full of preconceived ideas about what a Zen master should be. I had read what was available on Zen in English at the time, but knew nothing about Buddhism as it was actually practiced in Japan. Little by little my preconceptions were to dissolve as a result of the teachers I met and the community of Westerners and Japanese monks with whom I practiced. The dissolution of those preconceptions was the beginning of real learning for me.

A small community of Westerners came to Kyoto to practice Zen meditation at Antaiji, a temple in a northern suburb of the city. This is a story of those students, Uchiyama Kōshō, the abbot of Antaiji, and four other Zen teachers whom I learned of through my connection with Antaiji.

Four of those teachers were priests—three from the Sōtō Zen sect and one from the Rinzai Zen sect—and one was a laywoman Zen teacher. Each taught their own distinctive brand of Zen, different from the Zen of others and from the teachings of the orthodox Rinzai and Sōtō Zen establishments of their times. Yet they shared one essential thing: a strong commitment to zazen, or Zen meditation, a true love of the practice that utterly surpassed the lip service given it by so many Zen Buddhist priests in Japan of their day.

Kōshō Uchiyama, abbot of Antaiji, is the central figure in this story. Uchiyama was a Sōtō Zen priest who created an atmosphere at Antaiji that welcomed people from all walks of life to practice Zen meditation. Many Westerners found their way to Antaiji as a result of Uchiyama's openness. Perhaps the best-known of the Zen teachers I have focused on is Kōdō Sawaki, Uchiyama's teacher and a maverick Zen master who traveled the country preaching zazen. Though Sawaki was officially the abbot of Antaiji during the latter part of his life, he never actually took charge of a temple and was nicknamed "Homeless Kōdō." Sawaki is also the human link that connects each teacher to the others.

Sodō Yokoyama was a lone monk who spent his days sitting in zazen, playing songs by blowing on a leaf, and brushing poems that he composed in his "temple"—a public park he visited daily. He was a disciple of Sawaki for over thirty years. Kōzan Kato was a close friend of Sawaki and the only Rinzai Zen master in the group. He became known in Japan in his ninety-fourth year when a Japanese Buddhist teacher and scholar published a taped account by Kōzan of his life and Zen philosophy. His total disregard for fame earned Sawaki's respect.

Motoko Ikebe, a laywoman disciple of Uchiyama, is the sole woman Zen teacher in my story. This was a feat in itself in the overwhelmingly male-dominated world of Japanese Zen. She lived a simple life in a country village in Hyōgo Prefecture, and her quiet demeanor and strongly charismatic presence attracted many students to seek her guidance. She had them all practice zazen and advised in many other aspects of their lives as well.

As I set these stories down, I found myself writing more and more about my relationship with Uchiyama and the community of Zen students with whom I practiced. Many of the anecdotes recount how we lived and practiced around Antaiji, and may not be directly related to formal Zen meditation practice; what they do show is how a group of people who came to Japan to study Zen lived and worked and played while trying to maintain a meditation schedule created by Uchiyama at Antaiji.

Like our teacher, we believed in the inherent wisdom of meditation practice but we also realized that following that practice did not make us "special." For Uchiyama, practicing Zen was not something people did in a vacuum, in a protected environment free of the demands of the world around them. He wanted his monks to devote ten years to monastic practice before returning to Japanese society, but he also believed that, even while they were training at Antaiji, they should not be completely isolated from life outside of the monastery. He was happy to have Western men and women practicing at Antaiji, believing that the cross-cultural contact would be good for the monks as well as the Westerners. And he never encouraged any of the Westerners to take monastic vows, though some did. Uchiyama wished to eradicate the exotic and the mystic from Zen practice and show us that Zen was life in the world—but with a greater degree of sanity.

When I lived at Antaiji during my first months in Japan, there were Sunday zazen meetings for the local Japanese lay community. One man, who spoke some English and probably wanted to practice it, struck up a conversation with me. What he told me illustrates the atmosphere Uchiyama hoped to create for his students. "When I met the Roshi in a private meeting yesterday," he said, "I told him that I sit zazen for an hour in the morning and an hour in the evening. I then asked him if there was anything else I should be doing as a lay Buddhist practitioner. He said to me, 'You should be a good father and a good husband.'"

In an attempt to give the readers a more complete picture of my subjects, I have tried to tell their stories from as many different perspectives as possible, drawing freely on a wide variety of materials, first-person and otherwise, in English and Japanese . For example, I have told the story of Sodō Yokoyama, the poet-monk who composed music that he played on a leaf, through the eyes of many different people. Some, like his brother-disciple Uchiyama, wrote articles about him, and I've included samples of them. Yokoyama also told his own story in a book of his collected writings edited by his only disciple, Jōkō Shibata; I've included excerpts from that collection as well. And finally, my meeting with Yokoyama and interview with his disciple, Shibata, many years later, add to the picture, providing a comprehensive and multifaceted description of this remarkable man.

Uchiyama's distinct approach to Zen set the tone for practice at Antaiji and the attitudes of his students. Those who preferred other ways of practice left; those that stayed were of a certain bent. Like the teachers in the book, we believed in the importance of Zen meditation above all other aspects of Zen Buddhism. We also valued a certain amount of independence in our lives. Life at and around Antaiji under the guidance of Uchiyama allowed us to pursue both our commitment to meditation and our personal freedom.

Zazen was the focus of all the teachers in this story. Their faith in it and their stress on it over other aspects of Buddhism (though they certainly did not disregard those other aspects) is the common link here. I have attempted to give a picture of as many aspects of the lives of the teachers, the community and the temple as possible, but the essential story is that of five Zen masters living and dying in zazen.

This is a story of friendships; friendships that go beyond the story. I continue to get help from those among whom I lived in Japan and elsewhere over the years. Steve Yenik, Mike Hofmann, and Tom Wright, who gave me support throughout my stay in Japan, continue to be there for me when I need friends. They have been available throughout the production of this book to answer questions and fill in where my memory has failed. Steve took the first draft of the manuscript and went through it carefully, making many suggestions and corrections. I don't think I would have had the confidence to continue if he hadn't taken it upon himself to devote so much time to my work. Mike also read through the manuscript and helped me greatly with his perceptive comments. Tom read portions of the story making valuable suggestions.

Don Sweetbaum, a friend since childhood, read the first draft and made wonderful suggestions; his ear for language proved invaluable. Ralph Edsell, always willing to read my writing, encouraged me with helpful comments. Stuart Lachs read sections one and three and helped me greatly with his sense for detail and his deep understanding of Zen. Lee Nichol encouraged me to write more about the cross-cultural aspects of my life in Japan. I have always valued his advice greatly. Diana and Richard St Ruth allowed me to reprint sections from articles I wrote in *Buddhism Now*. Their constant support is greatly appreciated.

Reverend Jōkō Shibata opened his home to me for long discussions about his teacher Sodō Yokoyama Roshi. Reverend Taigan Katō gave me books about his father, Kōzan Katō Roshi, and answered my many questions about his father's life. He also made available to me photographs of Katō Roshi. Reverend Dōyū Takamine described Kōdō Sawaki Roshi's lecture, which he attended as a junior high school student. The description brought Sawaki Roshi to life for me. Reverend Shōhaku Okumura shared his understanding of Sawaki and Uchiyama Zen and his memories of life at Antaiji.

When I needed photographs for the book and had little time before production, I called to Japan and was helped in a pinch by Katō Roshi's family, Tom Wright, Reverend Shūsoku Kushiya, Hirotoshi Koyama of Daihōrinkaku Publishing Company, Yoshiharu Mizuno, Shūko Ikebe, and Munehiko Maeda.

My partner, Hiroko, is my severest critic and biggest help. She read through the stories and never let up until they read to her satisfaction. She was always there for me, and ready to answer my questions about confusing passages in the Japanese. Our daughter Nao, the real writer in the family, made valuable suggestions.

Finally, I want to thank my editor Jeff Hunter at Weatherhill for his patience and hard work making a manuscript into a beautiful book.

I SODŌ YOKOYAMA

A camellia blooms on the eaves edge
Of Antaiji's shrine
Petals scatter on the verandah

—Sodō Yokoyama

ANTAIJI TEMPLE

The train emerges from the underground at Kyōbashi Station, the last stop in Osaka on this limited express. Daylight floods the car. I put down my book and look out the window. Tall city buildings spattered with flashy advertisements give way to simple private homes, family shops, and rice paddies. As we approach Kyoto, dark-wood traditional homes nestled together on the East Mountain, red torii gates, one after the other, climbing this green slope to Inari Jinja, the shrine to the fox god, and the tall roofs of the Tofukuji Temple buildings transport me to a medieval Japan, a time when this city was its capital.

When we move into downtown Kyoto the train is once again underground. The windows are like dark mirrors. Two young Westerners, board the train. I don't realize how much I stand out in this homogenous culture until I see other gaijin—the Japanese word for foreigner. We notice each other but pretend not to: they by looking down, and I by peering out a black window. The number of Westerners grows significantly each time I return to this city, and we seem to grow shyer in each others' presence. But it is not only the numbers. Most of the foreigners in Kyoto in the early seventies were wanderers and bearers of an exciting new consciousness. We would strike up conversations with each other on trains or in coffee shops. 'These people don't look like dharma bums. But then again, neither do I. Are they exchange students, businessmen, or simply tourists?

I get off at Kitayama Station and walk fifteen minutes to my friend Mike's house, where I will stay for a few days. It is early July, and this short walk is enough to drench me in sweat.

"Hey Arthur, come on in." Mike greets me at the door. Looking at my wet shirt, he asks, "Want to take a shower?"

His shower is a hose with a spray nozzle that extends from his kitchen sink out the window into a small concrete front yard with a drain in the middle of the yard. Public baths are dying out in Japan because more people are putting baths in their homes. As fewer people use the public bath, the price goes up. I appreciate Mike's offer, but the anticipated joy of soaking in a large tub—some are as big as an average bedroom—is already occupying my mind. And I didn't bring many changes of clothing.

"Not now," I say.

Mike shows me his recent paintings and we have tea.

"How's Jikihara after his stroke?" I ask.

Mike's art teacher is in his late nineties. Their relationship goes back almost thirty years, to the time Mike first came to Japan.

"He's doing fine. He gets around in a wheelchair now, but he's still painting. When he gets tired, he sometimes asks me to finish his painting for him. He got mad at me the other day."

"What happened?"

"He was finishing a painting of a large tree. He got tired and asked me to finish it for him. I was painting the leaves too large. He said it made the tree look tiny. I'd never thought of it that way before."

"What did you do?"

"I just made them smaller, that's all."

After tea I ask him if he would like to take a ride to Gentaku.

Though not particularly tall for an American, Mike walks with his head constantly bent to keep from banging into crossbeams from the low ceiling of this traditional house. He pushes some brushes to one side, rolls up a few paintings, wipes some crumbs off his little multipurpose table, and hands me a motorcycle helmet. His house is about five minutes south of Gentaku.

Mike maneuvers his motorcycle through parked bikes and potted plants in front of small, graceful houses crowded tightly together. This narrow alley opens into a bustling shopping area. Shops display their goods on the sidewalks and there's a flood of people and bicycles, all on the move.

Gentaku is the name of an area and a street in the northern part of Kyoto. It is where Antaiji Temple used to be, and visiting the remains of the temple is the object of my trip. We ascend Takagamine Street, houses and stores shoulder to shoulder as I remembered them being twenty-five years before. But when we turn on to Gentaku Street, the houses nestled together covering the length of the street are definitely not part of my memories. When I first entered Antaiji, this area was mostly rice fields and vegetable gardens, with only a scattering of houses.

"You recognize this place?" Mike asks, watching for my reaction.

I turn toward a two-story apartment house with eight units. There are buildings on all four sides of it and a narrow path leading to the entrance. Though it once had rice paddies on one side and open spaces on two others, I have no difficulty recognizing it.

"Tsuchihachisō," I reply, the name of a small apartment complex—one of two that housed many foreigners who were practicing at Antaiji in the early 1970s. It was Mike's first home when he arrived in Kyoto. I'm already feeling some of the excitement that I felt when I first came to Kyoto in 1969. We arrive at the bus shelter where Takagamine and Gentaku streets meet. A little farther down I notice a man carrying a wooden box with a long handle. Takuro-kun!

Mike stops the bike.

Standing across the street from us is a chubby little man with a big smile revealing his sole remaining tooth. He only had one tooth when I saw him at Antaiji many years back. In fact, everything about Takuro-kun looks the same: his pants a little too high on his waist, his shirt half tucked in, and his hair uncombed. I thought he was in his forties then, and after twenty-five years, he still looks like he's in his forties. I remember him dropping by Antaiji often, joking with the monks and the foreigners. He was a little child mentally and the monks were always gentle with him.

As Takuro-kun turns and looks at us, something about us seems to register with him and his face lights up.

"Where you going?" he asks.

"We're checking out the old Antaiji."

He cocks his head and says: "Antaiji? Antaiji's gone."

"We're going to what's left of the temple," I say, but I can see by his expression that he doesn't understand.

Waving goodbye, Mike starts up the bike and we continue down Gentaku Street.

"Antaiji's gone," Takuro-kun repeats as we drive off.

Takagamine (Hawk's Peak) Street and Gentaku Street meet in the northwest corner of Kyoto atop a small hill overlooking the city. From that bend Takagamine Street continues north to the beautiful temple Kōetsuji, famous as an ancient hermitage for poets and scholars and popular for its venerable tea garden and rich autumn colors. Gentaku Street veers to the east, arriving at Shakadaniguchi, Entrance to the Valley of Buddhas, where another temple once stood: Antaiji. A poor shabby temple, Antaiji was known not for its classic beauty but for its founder and the fact that many foreigners practiced zazen with the resident monks and lived in or nearby the temple.

I want to see the old neighborhood and the memorial to the Zen master Kōdō Sawaki. This is the first time I've been back to this part of town since retuning to the States in 1977.

Mike stops the bike again and we get off near where we think Antaiji was formerly located. Though the area is crowded with houses, the heat of the afternoon keeps most people indoors. A middle-aged woman walks out of her house. I know by her casual attire that she isn't going very far. I approach her.

"Excuse me, how long have you been living here?"

The question startles her as much for the fact that it is a foreigner standing in front of her as for its personal nature.

"We built this house about fifteen years ago, but we lived nearby for many years before that," she says nervously.

"Do you remember Antaiji, the temple that stood where your house is?"

Having gotten over the initial fear of speaking to a foreigner, and realizing that we can converse in Japanese, she relaxes a bit.

"Yes, I remember it."

Mike stands on the side watching us.

I explain that we are trying to remember where the entrance to Antaiji stood. She listens politely and goes on her errand. Mike and I continue working on this time-space puzzle. We erase buildings that were newly built and replace them with remembered images of twenty-five years earlier. While continuing our investigation, the woman returns from the corner store carrying a small bag of groceries. Excited about this unexpected change in her daily routine, she joins us, and together we agree on the place where the entrance stood. Then Mike and I move on to the only thing that remains of Antaiji.

A stone under a maple tree, which was once a part of the garden adjoining the abbot's room, now lies in a fenced-off piece of land next to a prefab Jehovah's Witnesses church. It is a monument to the memory of Kōdō Sawaki Roshi, the well-known twentieth-century Zen master who became abbot of Antaiji toward the end of his life.

This unusual temple has a most unique beginning. It was first established in 1949 as a research center for the works of the Zen master Dōgen, founder of the Sōtō school of Zen Buddhism. Sawaki had been a professor at Komazawa University, the major college of the Sōtō Zen sect, and was given charge of the temple, and Antaiji became a temple with practitioners but no parish. When Sawaki died, his disciple Kōshō Uchiyama inherited the temple to do with as he saw fit. All he had to do was devise a way for it to survive financially—the typical temple in Japan being supported by its parish. Antaiji supported itself by donations from lay practitioners and by *takuhatsu*, a traditional form of almsgiving in which monks walked the streets with their begging bowls. This custom is still practiced in Zen monasteries in some parts of Japan.

Antaiji became a temple for students to practice Zen without the distractions most temples in Japan took for granted—parishioners needs such as funerals, memorial services, religious holidays, and in some cases weddings. At Antaiji, the resident monks took care of the temple grounds, practiced zazen or Zen meditation, and engaged in takuhatsu. The only ceremonies at the temple were the ordination of monks and lay persons and the yearly memorial service for Sawaki.

In the late 1960s a number of Westerners interested in cultures of the Far East traveled through Japan, and some found their way to Antaiji. If they were willing to follow the daily schedule of five hours of zazen, work around the temple grounds, takuhatsu, and participation in monthly five-day intensive retreats, they were welcome to stay at the temple. Most of the more prestigious official monasteries didn't accept Westerners at all; others only accepted those with intensive training in Japanese and temple etiquette and with formal introductions. But all were welcome to practice at Antaiji. The majority of Westerners practicing at Antaiji lived outside the temple, supporting themselves teaching English part time. They didn't necessarily participate in the daily life at the temple, but usually took part in the monthly intensive meditation retreats known as *sesshin*, which Uchiyama always stressed as the heart of the practice.

Antaiji was by no means a Shangri La, and Uchiyama was no saint, but Uchiyama did one thing that no other Zen teacher in Japan that I know of did—he created a place where Westerners could practice in a fashion similar to Japanese monks under the tutelage of a Zen teacher and with the help of a Zen community. There were other places where one or two Western practitioners who had become monks and had the proper introductions could practice, but the Westerners were usually a "curiosity" among a community of Japanese monks. At Antaiji, the community of monks and lay Japanese disciples worked together with a community of Westerners who were monks, laymen, and laywomen. Its probably true that early on neither group really understood the other very well, but a mutual understanding did grow with time. The Japanese monks were the community's leaders of course, but they knew that their teacher respected people who traveled eight thousand miles to practice with them, and so they felt compelled to be tolerant at the least, and many of the monks genuinely respected the Western practitioners.

I came to Japan in June 1969 with a desire to study Zen. All I knew of the subject came from a few popular books by Alan Watts and D. T. Suzuki that I had been reading while living in Nigeria, where I was a U.S. Peace Corps volunteer teaching math and science at a small school in the northern part of the country. I spent all my spare time reading, mostly books on spiritual and philosophical subjects. When my two-year period of service was over, I knew that I wanted to see Asia and experience Zen first hand. At that time there were many Westerners roaming the East with similar ideas.

That August, I found myself walking the streets of Kyoto looking for a place to practice. I had come from a small temple in Tokyo called Tōshōji run by a teacher named Tetsugyū Ban. Ban Roshi had accepted me into his temple and taken a couple of disciples and me to a sesshin in Morioka, a town in Northern Japan. That was the first time I had heard the word "sesshin," and my interpreter mistakenly described it as a meeting of Buddhists discussing religious topics. Soon after we arrived at the temple, we were taken to a Zen meditation hall to do zazen. I was told to continue repeating the famous *koan* "*mu*" ("nothingness" or "not") until I had a "breakthrough," which was referred to in Zen as *kenshō* (seeing into your own nature). Koans are statements, usually by past Zen masters, pointing to ultimate truth. Following my orders, I sat in a meditation hall screaming the word "mu" at a frenzied pace while imagining with all my might that it was coming from my *hara*, a place in the lower abdomen below the naval. I was not the only one making this racket; half the people in the hall were making similar noises. It felt more like an institution for the mentally ill than what I had always imagined a meditation hall to be.

Sitting on my right was Tesshō, a husky monk with a large face and thick eyebrows resembling those of the ancient Buddhist master Bodhidharma. He too was growling *mu*, but there was something different in the way he was approaching it: he seemed to be doing it for my sake. Yes, that was it; he was mu-ing to show me how to do it, on the out breadth, deep from the hara. Apparently Tesshō had been assigned to take care of me through the sesshin. He spoke little English, though more than any other of Ban's disciples. From the time we left Tokyo on the day-long trip north to Morioka, he remained by my side with his English-Japanese dictionary, diligently searching for the right words while informing me of what was happening around us.

Even in *dokusan* (a formal meeting with the Roshi, when he tests the practitioners understanding of his koan), Tesshō was by my side with his dictionary, struggling to find the words to enable me to understand the teacher, and the teacher to ascertain my progress with the koan. He kneeled by me when I was in line for dokusan, encouraging me to keep mu alive deep inside my hara. At one point I broke down when the *tantō*, the assistant to the Roshi, smacked an old woman in front of me on the *dokusan* line. I walked away, ready to quit sesshin, but Tesshō coaxed me back saying, "The end is near, the end is near."

Tesshō was there, too, when Ban Roshi, after testing me with some "check points," said I'd solved mu. I'd come back to the dokusan line feeling a huge burden lifted from me. Ban Roshi interpreted this as kenshō, an initial *satori* or awakening, but in fact it was merely the break in the tension I'd been feeling through the three days of sesshin—back and knees aching while trying to follow the proper sesshin behavior—that came when I cried at the absurdity of this old lady getting smacked with the *kyōsaku*, the "encouraging stick."[1]

When I told Tesshō on the ride back to Tokyo that Ban shouldn't have given me credit for kenshō, he agreed. I didn't know then that he was planning to leave Ban's temple to find a more authentic Zen master. This was the beginning of my friendship with Tesshō, a friendship that was to continue to this day. He is a friend and a wonderful advisor in matters of Zen, and he was happy when I told him that I was going to Kyoto in search of another teacher.

In this state of mind I came to Kyoto and walked into the first Zen temple I saw. The priest in charge looked at me as if I were crazy, then called a boy, perhaps a student of his, and asked him to take me to Antaiji. Antaiji had already developed a reputation for housing eccentric Westerners. A young monk named Ippei, who spoke English, met me at Antaiji's gate and led me to Uchiyama's room. Uchiyama, with a warm smile on his face, started the conversation.

"Welcome to our temple. What brings you here?"

"I came to practice Zen. I have just come from a temple in Tokyo. I was confused about the practice there so I left."

"How did they practice?"

I explained my experience at the sesshin in Morioka.

"Did you have a kenshō?" Roshi asked with a kind of chuckle.

"I did get credit for it, but it didn't feel like enlightenment. I even received something in writing."

"That I would like to see," he said as his chuckle turned into a laugh.

I started to laugh too. The informality of the meeting put me at ease.

"Kenshō is a game," he said. "Forget about it. Here we just sit."

He thanked me for joining them, and we bowed to each other. That was the beginning of my relationship with Antaiji and Uchiyama, and a teaching that I think I am only now, twenty-eight years later, really beginning to appreciate.

---

[1] Known as a kyōsaku in Sōtō Zen and a *keisaku* in Rinzai Zen. I have used both terms, following this distinction.

After a month at Antaiji I returned to the States. I wanted to see my family and to work and save enough money to return to Japan for an extended period of time to practice Zen. I taught mathematics in New York City for the following year, saving money and planning my return trip to Japan. In June of 1970 I wrote Uchiyama asking him if I could live and practice at Antaiji. He wrote back welcoming me to join them and everything seemed in place.

When I returned to Japan, I was welcomed to Antaiji by Uchiyama in his warm and simple manner, with little formality. I was happy to have found a temple with a teacher who had a sound approach to practice. At Antaiji rituals were kept to a minimum and the life there appeared to be designed to allow people every opportunity to practice zazen. Uchiyama kept traditional ceremonies and sutra recitation to a minimum, allowing more time for concentrated zazen.

At first I was euphoric at having found a place to practice the authentic way of the Buddha. As my excitement died down, I had the opportunity to observe real practice, but instead I chose not to look, and I started finding fault with my surroundings. Was Uchiyama the real McCoy? His less glamorous habits stood out. Why did he smoke? Why did he seem nervous when he spoke to us? Though marriage was common among Zen monks in Japan, I didn't want him to be married. I suppose I didn't want to think of him as an ordinary Zen monk.

When his teacher died, Uchiyama said that he would teach for ten years and then retire. I didn't think that Zen masters retired. My image was that of a Bankei (1622–93) or a Huangbo (J., Obaku, d. 850), patriarchs of Japan and China, whose lives were devoted exclusively to teaching and practicing Zen. Did they retire? I mulled over questions like this, bringing them up when I got together with friends who formed an informal international Zen community around Antaiji.

"What's wrong with retiring?" was Steve's response.

Steve had been in the community over a year before I arrived and I respected his opinion. It didn't seem right, I thought, but if it made sense to him, maybe I should give myself more time to live with the idea. I remember meeting my friend Tesshō again at Tōshōji on my way through Tokyo on my trip back to the States. I told him that I had met Uchiyama and had spent a few weeks sitting at Antaiji. He said that he had read Uchiyama's books and thought he was a genuine Zen teacher, so I stayed at Antaiji long enough to see Uchiyama in a new light, the way he deserved to be seen.

Uchiyama was an honest man. He warned us not to regard him as anything special, that he was no holy man. I am grateful now for his forthrightness, though I didn't understand it then. He never tried to fool anyone and, as a result, I haven't had to deal with some of those disappointments that plagued students of so many

Zen centers in America. He told us to look on zazen and not him as our teacher, and he really meant it.

When we sat sesshins, Uchiyama sat facing the wall like the rest of us. He didn't feel he should be directing us, but rather that he should be sitting with us. The practice would do the rest. Sometimes during sesshins I would get tired or frustrated or lonely, and I would glance through the corner of my eye at his cushion. The old man was sitting there with the rest of us—sometimes tired, head bobbing—but sitting, believing in the inherent power of the practice. It always gave me strength to see him sitting there, not as an overseer, but just sitting there, practicing as we did. No airs, just "Self being Self," as he would put it.

Uchiyama created a sesshin atmosphere at Antaiji that was unlike any I had experienced before or have experienced since, in Japan or in America. The way sesshins were run in this small Kyoto temple strikingly demonstrates his approach to Zen. No one was ever sent away for lack of space or funds. The temple could comfortably accommodate about thirty people. But there were times that it would seem to swell to house, feed, and provide sitting space for over a hundred. I'm reminded of a "Farmer Gray" cartoon I watched on TV as a kid. After emptying Farmer Gray's house of cheese and other goodies, a troop of mice went on a picnic, hundreds of them boarding a tiny bus. As they poured into the bus, it ballooned to many times its original size, and then when the mice arrived at their picnic grounds, they swarmed out of the bus and it shrank down to almost nothing. That's what happened at Antaiji sesshins, especially the ones around New Year.

Japanese traditionally pray at temples and shrines over the New Year's holiday; zazen practitioners like to sit in temples at this time. Many are working people who can't leave their jobs to sit for a full-length sesshin. The New Year sesshin started two days before New Year's Day and ended two days after. On December 31, people would start streaming into the temple, ready to sit and planning to spend the night. The meditation hall would fill with rows and rows of people covering every inch of floor space. Sitting cushions would appear and people would make room so that all of the space was used. A guest sleeping room, which could accommodate eight to ten sleeping mats, would sometimes have over twenty people in it, with people meeting for the first time squishing their bodies together to make room for newcomers. All this was done in relative silence. It was the strength of this one man and his will to make a place where all could practice that made it possible.

Uchiyama taught us through private meetings and lectured at specified times, but for him zazen was the highest teacher, and when we were doing zazen, he didn't want to interfere. I didn't understand his method then because I was too preoccupied with my ideal of an enlightened master. I was searching for a twentieth-century Bodhidharma. I had read about Ramana Maharshi, the saint of southern India, who sat in a cave absorbed in God while people built an ashram around him, and I wanted a teacher like I imagined the Maharshi to be.

There was a relative informality about Antaiji that made settling in far more relaxing than I imagine it would be at other Zen temples. To this day when I visit a Kyoto Zen temple, I enter with a bit of trepidation. This I believe is due greatly to the imposing architecture—these ancient wooden structures have a breathtaking beauty. When I visit them, I am in awe of their majesty, but I also feel a sense of relief when I leave and can relax again.

Antaiji had its own beauty. The bamboo grove along the path from the gate facing Gentaku, taking you into the temple grounds, helped you make the transition from your everyday working world to another kind of life. The meditation hall, though small, gave you the feeling of a structure from an ancient culture. But the rest of the buildings, with their patched screens and torn paper doors, told you that this was a place that was being lived in. Compared to buildings of the great Kyoto temples, Antaiji looked like a ramshackle hut. It quickly started to feel like home.

I spoke no Japanese when I arrived at Antaiji, so a lot of my energy was spent trying to figure out what to do next. Two other Westerners living at the temple then—a Canadian, Morley, and an American, "Kansas John"—helped me greatly. Morley was planning to stay for another month and John didn't seem to have a plan. They helped keep me aware of the schedule: zazen from 5:00 to 8:00 AM, breakfast from 8:00 to 8:30, a morning work period, lunch, an afternoon work period, dinner and zazen from 7:00 to 9:00 PM. But they spoke little Japanese and so were sometimes as lost as I was.

People showed up at Antaiji from all parts of the world with lots of ideas. One German fellow, a believer in Zen macrobiotics, arrived excited and quite talkative. He had been on the road for a while and had not been able to keep to the macrobiotic diet, he said, but when he was on the diet he hardly needed any sleep. This appealed to me because I was always looking for more time in my day. He seemed to think that Zen macrobiotics was a cure-all and went on about this fact through dinner up until evening zazen. He assumed that the monks would know all about this diet and didn't have a clue to the fact that Zen macrobiotics was virtually unknown to the world at large until, in the 1960s, a Japanese couple who subscribed to it came in contact with the hippie generation in America. He talked, and the few monks that understood some English listened politely until they could no longer keep their eyes open. At 10:00 PM we all went to sleep. I'd forgotten what happened after that until I read an account by Morley of the incident. According to Morley, the following morning the monks served bacon and eggs for breakfast and we never saw the fellow again. I'm sure the monks were not as disappointed as he was with what was probably a rare donation by one of Antaiji's neighbors.

Takuro-kun used to drop by during work periods or after lunch. He didn't come to practice zazen but rather to hang out with the monks. I loved watching these encounters. He seemed to be having a lot of fun. I felt in awe of the monks on these occasions; they were so at home with this little man whose appearance repelled me at first. Conversations with him were limited to simple questions and answers and some playful teasing. I don't know how it started or who started it, but at some point Takuro-kun would look at someone and lunge forward or pretend to throw a punch and then stop. This would be accompanied by:

"Punchy."

If you flinched, which newcomers to the game usually did, he would laugh and say, "Scared you, didn't I?"

He never tired of this game. We used to play it with him and try to get him to flinch. It was a playful way of communicating with him.

Tesshō came to visit me at Antaiji. There was so much to talk about, but my ability in Japanese and his in English limited what we could actually say. I learned that he had left Tōshōji and Tetsugyū Ban for good. I congratulated him. He walked around the temple with Dōjun, the acting head monk, and they seemed to get on well. That evening, I got permission to leave the temple and together with two couples, Steve and Arlene and Tom and Yūko, we went out to see an outdoor Noh drama at a Kyoto shrine.

Tesshō didn't seem interested in studying under Uchiyama at Antaiji and I didn't ask him why. I looked forward to the time when my Japanese had improved enough so that I could ask him questions about his life and his first encounter with Zen. We said our goodbyes and the next thing I heard from him was that he had entered Eiheiji, the major training temple of the Sōtō Zen sect.

Another fellow, an Australian named Lew, who had lived the previous year near Antaiji soon returned from his travels and joined us at the temple. Lew talked of an old monk named Sodō Yokoyama who, like Uchiyama, was a disciple of the late Kōdō Sawaki.

Sodō-san, as he was known to us, was Uchiyama's older brother disciple. He had lived at Antaiji for eight years together with Uchiyama before leaving for Kaikoen, a public park in the city of Komoro in the northern part of Japan's main island, Honshū. He was described to me as a monk who lived in the woods spending his days doing zazen, writing poems, and playing music by blowing on a leaf. Here, it appeared, was someone who lived like the monks of old.

Lew had seen Yokoyama the previous year when he came to Antaiji for the annual memorial service for his teacher Kōdō Sawaki. Lew agreed to take Steve and I to visit Yokoyama at the park. Before we left for the trip, I had learned from others who knew Yokoyama that he lived in a boarding house near the park. That put a damper on my romantic fantasy of a monk living in the woods following his heart. Still, a man spending his days doing zazen, playing music through a leaf, and writing poems had to be a far more interesting Zen character than the typical priest running a temple in Japan.

THE LEAF WHISTLING ZEN MASTER: SODŌ YOKOYAMA

I turn on my tape recorder and listen to a song about a brother who was killed on a battleship during the Second World War: "Think of my younger brother as the sea." The voice is Sodō Yokoyama's. It is not beautiful by conventional standards, but it has a depth of feeling like the blues of Son House and Robert Johnson. The voice stops and what has to be one of the funkiest instruments in the history of music takes over. Like Yokoyama's voice, it conveys something extraordinary.

Yokoyama plays a leaf by holding it against his lower lip with two fingers and blowing across its edge. The sound is high pitched and unpolished. It has the sound of a reed instrument that is a bit raspy.

○

"The leaf is truly difficult to play," he wrote. "Blow it and you will always get a sound. You'll get a sound, but the difficulty is making music. I like it because the leaf embodies the essence of the whole tree and also because it is not an actual musical instrument. It's like playing sandlot baseball or boys wrestling just for the fun of it. So playing the leaf is playing sandlot music. If you think in terms of playing authentic music, you'll stop playing the leaf. But if you play to give travelers a souvenir song to remember, it doesn't matter how you play. When you play the leaf, you'll usually be a little out of tune. That's where its very charm lies…"

How similar to Yokoyama's philosophy of zazen, in which he sits with deluded thoughts as a part of the nondeluded universe.

> *Floating cloud monk*
> *Plays leaf-whistle soulfully*
> *Chikuma River*
>
> —*Written by a traveler*

It wasn't too cold that autumn day in 1970, so we slept outside. Lew pulled his van to the side of the road and set up his bedding inside while Steve and I slept in sleeping bags on the grass. With a 500-cc engine, the car looked like a Volkswagen bus shrunk down to half its size. Lew did most of the driving and didn't appear bothered that the car seemed to lift off the ground every time we passed a normal-sized car going the other way. It took a little more than a day from Kyoto, mainly along narrow, winding, two-lane roads. We arrived in Komoro early the second day and found Kaikoen Park about eight or nine o'clock in the morning. We went to the spot where we were told the "NHK TV leaf-whistling monk" stayed. Someone from NHK, Japan's public television station, had recently come to interview Sodō Yokoyama, and that's how people at the park apparently referred to him from then on. He hadn't arrived yet. I was sure he would be there from about five in the morning and was disappointed to hear, "Oh, the NHK monk. . . . He usually arrives between ten and eleven."

We decided to go to a local store and pick up some food and tea for Yokoyama, as it is customary in Japan to bring a present, no matter how small, when visiting someone. We found a store where we bought a package of green tea and some fruit. When we returned, it was about eleven and Yokoyama was there. He was a thin man with narrow, classical features, sitting with legs folded, his bottom resting on the back of his ankles in formal seiza position, his torso straight and long, making him appear much taller than he was. He wore a monk's work clothes and a kind of black beret that I'd only seen before in drawings of the eighteenth-century haiku master Matsuo Bashō. His dress and his carriage were dignified in a way that suggested a traditional upbringing rather than a self-conscious propriety. A plastic overhang was tied to three trees to protect him from rain, and a little coal stove, a pot, an ink stick and brushes and writing paper were all set up. When he saw three foreigners from a distance, he picked up one of the leaves he had in a small bowl of water and started playing "Swanee River."

We walked up to a smiling Yokoyama and explained that we were from Antaiji. That set him immediately to talking about zazen.

"Zazen is the practice of the universe. Even a minute of zazen is fine."

While he was talking, he folded his legs, lowered his eyes and started practicing, as if to remind him of his subject.

"This life is easy," he continued. "I come here every day with the exception of three, when I go to Antaiji for my teacher's memorial. I vowed to do this for twenty years," he said.

"What do you plan to do after that?" Steve asked.

"Go somewhere and teach zazen," he said, and then added, "A resolution to sit in a wood for twenty years may seem strange today, but it was not uncommon years ago."

I couldn't help but feel that this man sitting here, sometimes playing the leaf, sometimes practicing zazen, interacting with people passing by in such an animated fashion, was not so much like the monks of old as like a work of art—a poem perhaps. It struck me that he was engaged in a kind of performance art, practicing and teaching at the same time.

Yokoyama talked about Walt Whitman, who along with Stephen Foster was one of his favorite Western figures. We gave him the fruit and tea. His eyes lit up when he saw the tea. He asked us to eat the fruit and said that he would accept the tea as a present. His sweetly childlike nature won me over, and my initial disappointment with his talkativeness and that he wasn't practicing zazen in the woods at five in the morning quickly faded.

A mother and two boys about seven and eight years old stopped by. The mother asked Yokoyama to play a song for them and he did. He responded to the mother, but he was focused on the two boys, whose presence seemed to delight him. He started to tease them, calling the older brother Tarō and the younger one Jirō, common names for first and second sons in Japan. When the younger insisted that his name was not Jirō, Yokoyama said, "Then you must be Tarō and your brother Jirō." When they both objected, he went back to calling the older Tarō and the younger Jirō. They kept objecting and he kept reversing the order, enjoying himself immensely. He then talked with them about school. The younger brother said he spent most of his time during school outside in the hallway, implying that the teacher threw him out of the class quite often. The three kids, Tarō, Jirō, and Sodō, were having a wonderful time together as several people gathered around.

Yokoyama played another request on the leaf. When a woman asked him how old he was, he told her he was nineteen. She smiled but didn't seem to know how to respond. She asked again and he repeated nineteen. She laughed nervously. Yokoyama was not simply responding flippantly with whatever came into his mind, as I was to realize when I read his writings. The following is from a piece entitled *Nineteen Springs*:

> I moved from Kyoto to Kaikoen in the city of Komoro to play the leaf for passing travelers in April of 1958 when I was fifty-two years old. Ten years later some travelers started to call me grandpa. Now old and young alike call me grandpa. Yet not even in my dreams do I think of myself as a grandpa. Leaf blowing is a child's activity. Grownups and older folk never blow the leaf. But people nowadays don't know that so they call me "the leaf-playing grandpa." The leaf-blowing mind is a child's mind. Because I play the leaf I can tell people I am fourteen years old.

I am often asked how old I am. It would sound strange if I said I was fourteen so I usually say nineteen. Nineteen is still young so I say nineteen. Vacation travel has become popular in recent years. At Kaikoen, too, groups of older men and women visit, and they listen to me blow the leaf. It never fails that at least one in the group asks me my age. I always answer "nineteen." This response makes the older people happy.

Old people want to feel young. So I tell them that they all must become nineteen. Once three women in their sixties came to this bamboo grove. After listening to me play, they asked my age. When I responded with nineteen, they were extremely happy. They said that they were traveling because the fact that they were getting old made them lonely. They had set off on their trip with the hope that it would help pick up their spirits. They told me that they were glad they came here.

Yokoyama and Uchiyama lived together at Antaiji for about eight years when their teacher Kōdō Sawaki was alive. Sawaki was well known throughout Japan as a scholar monk who preached Zen and practiced zazen in a manner one might describe as "just sitting." Dōgen Zenji, the founder of the Sōtō Zen School in Japan, called this way of sitting *shikan taza*. Sawaki traveled around Japan preaching and running sesshins at various temples and lecturing at Komazawa University, the leading Sōtō Zen University. Because of his unusual life style, he was referred to as "Homeless Kōdō," an epithet he seemed to enjoy. He saw zazen as the most important activity in life, and at the same time as nothing special. In his own words: "We don't practice zazen in order to get enlightened; we practice zazen being pulled every which way by enlightenment."

The one thing Sawaki seems to have clearly transmitted to his two elder disciples was the importance of zazen in their lives. Both agreed on this, each respecting the other greatly for his commitment to the practice. It is questionable, however, that either of them agreed on much else. They lived at Antaiji together for eight years, much of that time by themselves. A large temple for two people, their rooms were as far apart as they could be while still remaining under the same roof. Their worldviews, as well, appeared to be quite far apart.

Yokoyama was like Ryōkan[2]; he might see a child, get absorbed in playing with her, and forget what he went outside to do in the first place. When he wasn't playing with children, he was occupied with poetry, calligraphy, or leaf blowing: activities that, along with zazen, played a great part in his life.

---

[2] Taigu Ryōkan (1758–1831) Japan's lovable poet-monk who spent hours of his day playing with children.

Practical matters, like taking care of Antaiji's grounds, were not high on his list of priorities. From Uchiyama's perspective he appeared quite irresponsible—and from the point of view of getting things done, he was. Uchiyama felt responsible for maintaining the temple. An origami artist himself, he surely empathized with his older-brother disciple's love of the arts; but Antaiji had to be maintained, and no doubt he felt some resentment that most of it fell to him while Yokoyama played with children. Though Uchiyama made disparaging remarks about his brother disciple when Yokoyama wasn't around, when they did get together they displayed a warmth for each other that was infectious.

When I attended the memorial celebration on the anniversary of Sawaki's death in the early 1970s, I enjoyed watching these two old monks teasing each other. Uchiyama took a sip of sake, his face flushed red, and he appeared relaxed. Yokoyama didn't touch sake, but was his playful self as usual. They told old stories of life at Antaiji and displayed a real fondness for each other. Yokoyama played the leaf and sang a few songs and at some point in the evening Uchiyama brought out his latest origami. He retired early, around nine, and Yokoyama stayed up a little later singing with the monks. Then he retired and the other monks got drunk and noisy before the party was over.

Yokoyama and Uchiyama contributed articles to a magazine called *Tsukumo*. Uchiyama's article about Yokoyama, *The Fellow Playing the Leaf Whistle*, shows a deep warmth.

> A lone monk begging in the streets of Kyoto from 1949 to 1957 would suddenly take a leaf from a tree and put it in his mouth. Then you would hear the beginning of an unimaginably beautiful tune. You might see him leading a group of children, all walking to the tune of his leaf-playing—just like the Pied Piper of Hamlin. I'm sure there are many people in Kyoto who still remember this.
>
> While the children happily gathered around this monk, as children did around Ryōkan one hundred fifty years ago, he would suddenly cover his head with the wide black sleeve of his monk's robe, and the children would run away squealing in delicious fear. Those children must be near thirty years old today.[3] This monk was called the "Leaf-whistle Player" throughout Kyoto. He is my elder-brother disciple, Sodō Yokoyama. In 1957, Sodō-san left Kyoto and moved to Kaikoen park in the city of Komoro in Shinshū (the Japan Alps), the place he loved most. There he really threw himself into his unique lifestyle, practicing zazen in the forest,

---

[3] This article was written August 22, 1968.

playing the leaf, and creating and performing songs such as "Near the Old Castle in Komoro."

Sodō-san was born into a family of retainers for the Toyoma clan near the city of Sendai. From his youth he excelled in writing haiku, *waka,* and songs. Now his poetic sensibility, his leaf playing, and his zazen together have become an attraction that lifts the hearts of travelers. In this materialistic world, how heartwarming this elegant life style is. He has even appeared on TV. I'm sure many viewers seeing him on television, sitting in the park with the Japan Alps in the background, recognized the leaf-playing monk they knew from childhood.

I've seen Sodō-san two or three times since he left Kyoto. It's already more than ten years since he began this timeless life in the Japan Alps. I feel that he at sixty-three has developed this sophisticated Way to perfection. It delights me to think that this man is my older-brother disciple of Kōdō Sawaki—the teacher who was referred to as "Homeless Kōdō."

Last summer I went to visit Sodō-san. He was happy, and over a fire made from a few pieces of firewood he boiled tea and played host. The following are poems he wrote for me at that time.

> *More than mother and father*
> *More than brothers and sisters*
> *I love mountains and rivers.*
> *How pitiful.*
>
> *Mother and father*
> *Brothers and sisters*
> *Forgive me,*
> *A child without a home.*
>
> *In a field far from home*
> *I think solemn thoughts*
> *Of mother passed on*
> *Whom I will never see again!*

○

After visiting Sodō Yokoyama, I was anxious to talk to Tesshō again. My Japanese had improved enough to make me feel I could finally have a real conversation with him, one that wasn't spent thumbing through a dictionary searching for the right word, and then trying to remember why the conversation had started in the first place. I had the telephone number of his older brother's temple in Odawara, a town about half an hour from Tokyo. When I called to ask about his whereabouts, he happened to be staying with his brother and he invited me to visit. I was no longer living at Antaiji and was free to travel between sesshins. When I arrived, Tesshō's sister-in-law answered the door, and I introduced myself.

"Welcome Arthur. Masao has told me so much about you."

"Masao?" I responded with a puzzled look on my face.

"Oh, I'm sorry. Tesshō," she corrected herself. Masao was Tesshō's given name. She led me into his room and then disappeared.

Tesshō was sitting by a low table, books strewn on it and around the room. He looked up, cleared the books from the table, and said: "Arthur, thanks for making the long trip. You must be tired."

We talked while sipping cold barley tea that his sister-in-law quietly placed in front of us.

"You look thinner," I remarked.

"I just came off a ten-day fast."

Tesshō was the only monk I knew who seemed interested in Yoga, fasting, and any practice related to religion. He didn't need a meditation hall and a congregation to encourage him to practice; he did zazen wherever he was.

We had a lot to catch up on. "What have you been doing since leaving Tōshōji?" I asked.

"I spent six months training at Eiheiji. Then I heard about an abandoned shrine in the mountains in Yamanashi Prefecture and I went there to live. But I got into trouble. I fasted there for thirty days and when I came off the fast I had such severe constipation I thought I was going to die. I couldn't move and I didn't know what to do. After lying there for a day or so, I was finally able to relieve myself. As soon as I could move I came down here to stay with my brother and convalesce. I think I'll stick to ten-day fasts from now on."

I told him about my visit to Yokoyama, and I guess I shouldn't have been surprised when he said he knew of him.

"I thought about studying with him once, but I heard that he doesn't accept disciples."

"Well he has one disciple now, an ex-Antaiji monk named Jōkō," I said. "Apparently Yokoyama asked Jōkō to spend three years training at Eiheiji before joining Yokoyama in Komoro City."

"Three years at Eiheiji? I don't know how anyone can survive that."

That didn't sound like Tesshō. Hard practice was something he seemed to thrive on. "Is it that difficult?" I said.

"The first three months are okay. At the beginning you really train. But soon you become a senior and then all you do is harass others. That has nothing to do with training. Anyone serious about Zen would go crazy once he became a senior at that temple."

I should have known that for him it would be difficult to survive if he weren't training as hard as he could.

"Why don't you try to study with Yokoyama?"

"It's easy for you as a foreigner to go anywhere you want. You can walk into any temple and ask to meet the teacher. It's not that easy for we Japanese. Once we have taken ordination from one teacher, we can't simply move on to study with another."

I didn't push him further on that point, though I was surprised that he felt so restricted. We talked more about Tōshōji and Tetsugyū Ban, about Antaiji, and about my visit to see Yokoyama in Komoro. I asked him what his plans were, and he said he didn't know what he would do next. I spent the night there, we sat zazen together, and I left the next morning. All the way back to Antaiji I mulled over his lack of freedom in visiting Zen teachers. It seemed completely out of character for him, and I had also hoped that he would visit Yokoyama and give me his take on the man.

SODŌ YOKOYAMA'S ZAZEN

Sodō Yokoyama started practicing zazen after reading Dōgen's *Zuimonki* when he was twenty-two, and furthered his understanding under the guidance of Sawaki Roshi. But when he writes about zazen he often refers to influences from his childhood, from nature, and from his father. He describes himself as the type of child who became completely absorbed in each new interest: with geometry, for example, in his third and fourth year in elementary school and then with baseball when he lost interest in mathematics.

> In the third grade, my older brother decided to teach me arithmetic. He wanted to help me appreciate learning. He taught me fractions in my fourth year and the following year, my fifth, he said he would teach me algebra and geometry. He took out a thick book and showed it to me.... The diagrams inspired me and I felt uplifted. I said to myself, "I will be learning this next year, how wonderful, how lucky I am!" ...To this day I cannot forget how moved I was as a youngster in the fourth grade when those diagrams from the geometry book excited me so. However, my

brother enlisted in the army during my fourth year in elementary school. In my fifth year, I played baseball and lost all interest in studying. Just as I was inspired in my youth (by the geometry diagrams), the "diagram" of zazen later stirred me so that I will never lose sight of it. I came to the realization that this was something I would never give up.[4]

Elsewhere Yokoyama talks about his father's role in his loss of interest in academics. On one occasion his father found him reading a high school mathematics book for pleasure, and berated him, saying that the only use for academic knowledge was to succeed in this world. As far as the universe was concerned, study was no help at all. Whether Yokoyama's father actually used the word "universe" or not, Yokoyama frequently employed this term rather than "Buddha Dharma" (Buddhist Truth) in his writings as a means of transcending the category of religion and pointing to the all-encompassing nature that he attributed to zazen.

Though his explanation of zazen was relatively free of religious imagery, it was not without love and passion for the practice, and you felt this passion when you were around him, saw it in the many photos of him practicing zazen, and encountered it in his writings about zazen and the natural world. He learned the truth of zazen from the sunset, from a pheasant in the mountains, and from the many travelers who dropped in to his "temple under the sky" in the Japan Alps.

He loved to walk in the mountains. Describing his fixation with watching the sunset in his hometown, he wrote: "If the red sunset had stayed forever, I would have gone crazy. Because the sun sank and the lighted sky disappeared, I could descend the mountain with my mind at ease. One evening I received a hint from the setting sun that all creation is beyond thought. The setting sun knows nothing about the setting sun, but it is the setting sun."[5]

This lack of self-consciousness was, for him, a hint that all creation was beyond thought. He was reminded by this hint of the time he saw his father doing zazen when he was a little boy:

> One spring evening when I was seven, my father sat by the sliding paper doors and playfully showed me the zazen posture. "The Buddha practiced this way," he said. In my young mind, the Buddha [was a fellow who] practiced like my dad. That evening in our garden, crabapples were in bloom.[6]

---

[4] *Waga Tatsu Soma* (The Wood Where I Stand) (Tokyo: Kioin Publishing Company, 1982), 219.
[5] Ibid., 108, 109.
[6] Ibid., 107.

The story of Yokoyama is the story of his notion of shikan taza, or just sitting. He was a poet, a calligrapher, a composer, and a musician, but for him these talents all rested on the foundation of zazen. Zazen, he would stress, was the universe. You didn't have to change yourself in order to experience this zazen; all you had to do was sit and let it take its course.

No gain, the final goal of many Zen practitioners, was for him the entry point to zazen. No thought, he would say, was there even though you were thinking.

He believed that the form of zazen posture itself was mysteriously efficacious, which he regarded as affirmed by the natural world. Several times in his writing he refers to a traditional Japanese poem he composed that describes being observed by a pheasant when doing zazen in the mountains.

> *Years ago,*
> *Meditating in the mountains,*
> *A pheasant appeared*
> *And stared*
> *At my zazen.*

Yokoyama felt that the fact that the pheasant wasn't afraid of a human being, as it normally would have been, confirmed his feeling that the form of zazen was perfect. "Had I lifted my eyes and looked at the pheasant," he wrote, "it would have flown away. So I kept my eyes lowered, my gaze four feet in front of me, and never looked up at it." He mentioned this incident to a friend and advisor, a Doctor Saito from Kumamoto, who had studied for many years with Sawaki. The doctor told him that animals will never look into the eyes of people because of the delusion they saw there. Yokoyama interpreted this as a confirmation of his view that the zazen posture, specifically the placement of one's line of vision while sitting, possessed a power that transcended the mind of the sitter.

> These eyes, this posture in zazen where the line of sight falls in front, is called *jigenshishujō* (compassionate eyes beholding all).[7] At that time I finally grasped these words. Though I didn't look at the pheasant while I was doing zazen, it was in my peripheral vision. Not looking at the pheasant showed an absence of evil intentions. This is the same as not looking at the evil in others. If you don't look at the evil in others, you are free.[8]

---

[7] This phrase comes from the next to last line in a verse section of chapter 25 of the Lotus Sutra, "Universal Gateway of the Bodhisattva Perceiver of the World's Sounds."

[8] *Waga Tatsu Soma*, 228–29.

The logic here—that not looking directly at someone would show an absence of evil intentions—I find questionable, but the point is that Yokoyama experienced a power from this practice that arose spontaneously and without effort on his part—a phenomenon very similar to the "other-power philosophy" of the Jōdo Shinshū (True Pure Land) Buddhists.

Yokoyama felt powerless to deal with the outside world, the adult world of profit and loss. He felt inadequate in that world and found affirmation of these feelings in the life of the eighteenth-century Zen monk Ryōkan. One of the most beloved figures in the history of Japanese Zen, Ryōkan refused to accept the hereditary position of village headman that his father sought to pass down to him. Instead he shaved his head and underwent Zen training. But in that realm, too, he refused to follow the prescribed path of administering a Zen monastery and training monks. Uncomfortable in any establishment, whether secular or religious, he lived alone in a thatched hut, begging for food. On rainy days, he stayed in his hut reading the Chinese classics, composing and writing poetry, and meditating. On clear days he begged from town to town, talking and drinking with farmers and playing with children.

When Yokoyama decided to "leave the world," he knew that he was no more prepared for a leadership role in Zen than he was for one in the secular world. He found in this eighteenth-century monk, who had become famous for his poetry, calligraphy, and simple lifestyle, a role model. Here was someone who had given legitimacy to the type of life he had chosen for himself. In a letter to a friend and mentor, he wrote candidly about these feelings:

> In the afternoon of the sixteenth of February, while walking down Takagamine Street I dropped and broke something I was to deliver to Sawaki Roshi in Ikeda City. There was nothing to do but return to Antaiji and ask myself how I could be so careless. At that point I realized that this was "me." In the record of Unkyō Roshi it is written: "Even when you are walking on the street or washing your face, don't forget the absolute."
>
> I returned to the temple, pondering this. Though I was careless then, there is a saying, "Though he be stupid, he is the heir," and another, "the dunce heir." To me this meant that the foolish are the true heirs to the universe. I had no qualifications that would entitle me to receive a paycheck. Not even being qualified to run the weaving business,[9] I put on black robes and left the world [became a monk]. This is who I am.
>
> I didn't want to run a weaving business. If I were to work the loom, I wanted to do it during the day and practice zazen at night. Wandering

---

[9] Sodō's family had a weaving business run by his older brother's family.

with no home is not easy, so I chose to work at my brother's loom for free in return for room and board. I explained these plans to my brother and asked him to build me a Zen meditation room;[10] I would work the loom during the day and practice zazen in the evening, spending the rest of my life in my hometown, Kitakamigawa. My brother said that he would agree to this but he could provide me with only two meals a day instead of three. I felt two meals a day would be fine. Now that I had decided to spend the rest of my life near Kitakamigawa, I thought I should attend at least one Zen meeting and receive traditional teaching in zazen. This was how I came to meet Sawaki Roshi and the reason I became a monk.

When I thought about who I was, I realized that I could never be a respectable man of the world. If I couldn't be a respectable man of the world, I couldn't be a respectable monk either. That's why I'd never considered becoming a Zen teacher, and I disliked scholarship for the same reasons. But I had determined the path I would take. I had no need for what others possessed, so I had no desire to devote myself to study.

Ryōkan was a truly genuine monk in Japan yet he couldn't get along in the world. He certainly wasn't a respectable man of the world. So even as a monk he chose not to be a temple master. He knew he couldn't. That's why he lived as he did. Still he did perfect the myriad things in the world of the heart.

Based on this tradition, I saw zazen as "a posture bestowed upon me by the Buddha." The myriad things then became "beyond thought" and home became a sacred place. . . . Whether people of the world practiced it or not, zazen was the way of the world, the way of the universe. The way beyond thought was the way of the world.

I awoke to this wisdom of the Buddha Way completely, and in accord with the tradition set down by Ryōkan, I donned black robes and decided to pass through this world as a monk. While Ryōkan played ball, my way was to keep the zazen posture from disappearing in Japan. First, I felt that I had to devote myself to keeping to this practice. Next I thought that I had to pass it on to others. I knew where to find people to transmit this practice. Near the old castle ruins in Komoro City among the groups of leisure travelers I thought there must be many. In my later years, I decided to reside in Komoro, near the castle ruins,

---

[10] During this period in Japan, the older brother received the family estate and was responsible for taking care of the family.

by the monument inscribed with Tōson [Shimazaki]'s poem. There I would introduce zazen to the groups of travelers and someone among them would embrace it. I truly believed that this plan would succeed. I was certain there wasn't anyone in this world without some interest in zazen. But first I had to keep this practice myself. The best way to preserve this practice was to follow my teachers maxim: "Make an offering of your body to zazen."

POEMS AND SONGS

Both Yokoyama and Ryōkan were ordained Sōtō Zen monks, but neither administered a temple or trained other monks. Instead, they both taught through the way they lived. Poetry played a major role in their lives, and in the end, their lives became their greatest poems.

> I first heard waka from my grandmother. When I was young, she talked to me about the old days. I can remember the first waka I read when I was a boy. It was on a winter day and the *Gensen Waka* collection from our bookcase fell into my hands and I read it by the *kotatsu* (foot warmer). It was, by chance, from the winter series. I thought it was quite good and, though unintentionally, I memorized it.
>
> > *Godless month*
> > *Raining on and off*
> > *Unpredictable season*
> > *Winter's beginnings.*

In 1929, Yokoyama read Dōgen Zenji's *Zuimonki* (Record of Things Heard). He was taken by the phrase: "If you pass your time sitting in 'no-gain, no-satori,' you will be practicing the Way of the Patriarchs (Sodō)." Later when he was ordained by Sawaki he was given the name Sodō.

In 1940, Yokoyama entered Sōjiji, one of the two head Sōtō-sect Zen temples. After training for two years at Sōjiji, he traveled west to Higo (present-day Kumamoto Prefecture) and entered a temple in Kumamoto City on the island of Kyūshū. There he became friends with Kumamoto no Kō, an accomplished calligrapher and *waka* poet. Under Kō's guidance Yokoyama started to compose waka poems. Kō read Yokoyama's poems and gave him advice. Yokoyama and Kō kept up a correspondence until the latter's death in 1973.

I had never composed waka until I entered the fields of Higo.... This poem "Under the root of barley" is the first I ever composed, so I created a melody to commemorate the occasion. It was the first song I'd ever written.

> *In the fields of Higo*
> *By the roots of barley,*
> *The flower of another plant*
> *Along with barley*
> *Was gathered in the harvest*

On June 5, 1942 Yokoyama learned of the death of his brother during a naval battle off the Bay of Midway Island.

> *Mother dear mother*
> *From now on*
> *Consider Neptune's Sea your child.*

> *The Sea of Midway Island*
> *Doesn't know of my brothers death.*
> *My brother doesn't know either.*

> *When I look at Neptune's blue sea,*
> *I see my brother;*
> *I want to pray to the sea.*

On October 31 of the same year, Yokoyama's mother died.

> *In a field far from my hometown,*
> *I think of my dead mother;*
> *The thought I will never see*
> *My mother again*
> *Fills me with grief.*

On March 7, 1946 Yokoyama learned of the unexpected death of his older brother.

> *Broad bean flower in the fields of Higo,*
> *My brother died suddenly*
> *By the Kitagami River.*

That same year Yokoyama moved from Higo to Fuōzan Temple in Tamba, where he first met Uchiyama.

> *A thought in Fuōzan Temple in Tamba*
> *"Life and death are one"*
> *Means no life or death.*

On April 10, 1948 Yokoyama moved from Tamba to Teishōji Temple in Shina (present-day Maeyama in Saku City).

> *I cross Chikuma River*
> *For the first time;*
> *Spring jewels crown the waves.*

In August 1949 Yokoyama moved to Antaiji in Kyoto.

> *Facing Asama Mountain*
> *Smoke rises;*
> *The sleeve of a traveler's robe flutters.*

> *I receive play money*
> *From a child;*
> *The joys of begging in the capital.*

> *I stand in front of a gate;*
> *Cosmos flowers bloom.*
> *Chanting hōōō*
> *With my begging bowl,*
> *Someone comes forth.*

> *Out begging,*
> *I stand in front of a flower shop.*
> *Rape blossoms bring joy to this winter day.*

> *Begging at Nishioji,*
> *Spring snow falls*
> *Wetting my umbrella and begging bowl.*

Just like last year at Nishiōji
Spring showers turn to snow
Falling on me.

Beautiful,
The evening sun in the sky
Over the edge
Of the school building
Shining.

The roof was damaged from the storm,
But the bush clover in Antaiji's garden
Is peaceful.

The joy of playing the leaf
In the shack of the temple
On top of Hawk's Peak.

At the entrance to Antaiji's garden,
Where there's a view of Mount Hiei,
A cosmos flower blooms.

Someone waits alone
At the Gentaku bus stop.
Insects swarm.

Evening of a day of snow flurries.
Piled high on Antaiji's roof
Melting snow.

Sasanqua flowers bloom again this year
Near Antaiji's shrine.
Pigeons fly away.

Near the eave's edge of Antaiji's shrine,
Sasanqua bloom.
Their petals scatter on the veranda.

Doing zazen—
I face the wall welcoming in the day.
I face the wall sending off the night.

An hour of morning zazen
With my Sendai nephew
At the foot of Kitayama Mountain.

I leave on a journey.
No zazen at Antaiji
For some time!

Living at the Gentaku temple,
A day doesn't go by
Without zazen.

Years ago,
Meditating in the mountains,
A pheasant appeared
And stared
At my zazen.

○

Kyūji Inoue was on the staff of Daihōrin, a large Buddhist publishing company in Japan. He wrote articles for the company's Buddhist magazine and was in charge of the art department. He interviewed many religious figures, and his article describing his visit to see Yokoyama gives a wonderful picture of Sodō's life in the park.

THE LEAF-PLAYING ZEN POET IN THE CASTLE RUINS AT KOMORO

The castle ruins in Tōson Shimazaki's poem "Near the Old Castle in Komoro" are now a park called Kaikoen. Stone fences still stand here and there about the site. Following the path between trees, with their patches of the autumn colors of early October, I found the object of my search in the shade of a thicket of bushes. At almost the same moment he seemed to notice me, and we waved to each other, also simultaneously.

"You recognized me from quite a distance," I said.

"Well, I've seen your face in *Daihōrin* magazine many times. Thank you for coming all this way. Please don't consider today work. Just think of it as a picnic."

Sodō Yokoyama Roshi, known here as the monk who plays the leaf whistle, laid a flattened cardboard box on the ground and placed a cushion on top of it.

"Please, take off your shoes and sit down. This is my dragon castle, and I'm Urashima Tarō."[11]

I must describe this dragon castle. On the north side is a bamboo grove, with a wood in the far background. The bamboo grove obstructs the winds in winter and is a perfect screen for the sun. Because of the positioning of the trees, we were in a kind of cul-de-sac, separated from where people walk.

This is where the dragon castle stood. In front of my seat, which I will call the guest's seat, there was a portable cooker. Roshi's seat was on the other side of the cooker. Dirt was piled high under the cooker to allow the water to drain off when it rains. Two areas near some bamboo clumps were lined with two or three sheets of old corrugated plastic and tin. Various pieces of equipment were packed together under the sheets, creating a sort of personal locker. My cardboard seat was taken from his personal locker, too. In addition, there were various knickknacks used for cooking, resembling an area where children play house.

"All you have to do is decide that wherever you are is the best place there is. Once you start comparing one place to another, there's no end to it."

Urashima Tarō was explaining why this particular place was his very own dragon castle.

"It's the same with your work. If you decide it's the best, then it is. Now let me pour some tea. The tea here is delicious."

My expectations were aroused, but the tea didn't come right away. At the bottom of the portable stove a piece of kindling coal remained. Roshi kept breaking twigs and adding them to the stove, and with a branch in the place of tongs, skillfully kindled a flame.

"Now while we wait for the water to boil. . . ."

---

[11] Yokoyama is referring to a Japanese folk tale whose hero, a young fisherman named Urashima Tarō, is led to a magical dragon castle beneath the sea. When he returns to his home on land, hundreds of years have passed.

Roshi took a leaf that was floating on the surface of water in a plate and with the tips of two fingers held it to his lips. The sound of the leaf as he played "The Song of a Traveler's Heart from Chikuma River"—a bit sad, artless, and occasionally faltering—resonated with the flow of the autumn air. Sitting on his ankles, knees folded, his left hand tapping the beat on his thigh, he continued with the tunes "Abandoned House from My Hometown" and "Clay House."

Water began to boil in a small, dented pot. A few people started gathering around. He stopped playing the leaf and put tea leaves in the pot with a graceful motion.

Placed on the ground in front of my cardboard mat was a piece of bark peeled from a tree trunk. On it were two pale cherry leaves side by side, serving as plates. On one lay pickled greens and on the other sweet boiled chestnuts. Two sticks of bamboo were used as chopsticks. How elegant, how refined a table he had set.

Under the soft beams of sunlight in the afternoon, Roshi's withered classical features somehow brought to mind the monk Ryōkan. But I couldn't immerse myself in those poetical sentiments. As many groups of visitors surrounded us and I was exposed to their line of vision, I became a little—actually, greatly—self-conscious.

At this time, a wonderful chorus sprung up in the wood from a group of women, and I thought, "A chorus here?" The song was "The Red Dragon Fly at Dawn." The voices and the sound of the leaf in harmony drew me in, and only then did I feel I had lost my self-consciousness.

"I practiced at the Sōtō Zen Temple Antaiji in Takagamine in Kyoto."[12]

"When you were a young man?"

"Around 1962, I was about fifty-two or fifty-three."[13]

This surprising revelation[13] made it difficult to ask anything more about his past.

"Well how old would that make you now?" and I started counting on my fingers.

"I'm always nineteen," he said laughing. "I was born on the first day of the ninth month of the forty-third year of Meiji [1907][14].... I used to think of my hometown when I went to bed at Antaiji. I would recite:

---

[12] Yokoyama was at Antaiji from 1949 to 1957.

[13] Fifty-two is quite old for someone in religious training.

[14] In fact he was born in 1904.

> *Autumn evening in bed thinking of my hometown*
> *I had a dream—dreamt of my hometown.*
> *Far north of the capital on an autumn evening*
> *I had a dream—dreamt of my hometown.*

"I was born near the Kitakami River."

He said he created a melody for it, then took it to his music teacher and had him refine it. Yokoyama sang the song in a deep, quiet, gentle voice. When he finished, he returned to his leaf, playing it over and over. Somewhere in a nearby tree top, a small unseen bird joined in.

"It was autumn. I had returned from begging and nobody was around. One person was assigned to guard the gate, but he was nowhere to be found. On the sliding door I had just repapered, the sun was shining from the west. A praying mantis had perched itself there. I felt as though the praying mantis had guarded the place for me, and I told it that we would frolic together. I quickly took off my straw sandals, washed my feet, and went to see it, but it was gone. Its watch was over so I guess it left. It became quiet."

Here Yokoyama sang another song:

> *It perched itself on a white sliding door I'd papered.*
> *Autumn's praying mantis, where has it gone?*

I could no longer see anybody nearby. Here too it became quiet. A stray cat cried and scattered away. I suddenly felt a chill in my legs and hips. The chill penetrated my body from the ground. It was four o'clock.

"It gets chilly around four o'clock. Lets prepare to go home."

Yokoyama soon began closing up the dragon's castle. Starting with the portable cooker, the various cooking utensils, and other knickknacks, he carefully put his two personal lockers back in order.

"Even if it rains, everything is safe under here."

Then he meticulously swept, put the food in carrying bags, took off his sandals and put on shoes, and we set out on the approximately two-kilometer road to his home. Though I had a place to stay in front of the train station, I accompanied him. Jōkō Shibata, a monk who was practicing under Yokoyama's guidance and had been monastery cook at Eiheiji, where he had practiced for three years, had invited me to join them in a vegetarian meal, and I gladly accepted.

Yokoyama lived together with this disciple on the bottom floor in the back of a two-story boarding house situated in a field outside of the town. It was a gloomy twilight evening. There were purple mushrooms, gingko nuts, and chrysanthemum petals—rare treats picked at Kaikoen Park. They were so delicious that even I, whose appetite has declined of late, found myself over-indulging. The more we ate, the more enlivened the conversation became .

"I didn't come here at first planning to live like this."

Yokoyama had first come to Kaikoen in Komoro around 1958.

"At the beginning I placed some paper under a pine tree and practiced zazen and played the leaf. It just naturally evolved to this. Even that spot took about six or seven years to decide on. At first I wasn't comfortable with it. The timing has to be right. You know, karmic connections."

This poetic priest from a fairytale said: "My temple is the Temple of Sun, Mountain, and Blue Sky, and this earth is my campground."

His world was not merely a dragon castle but more extraordinary, more sublime, more grandiose.

"Leaves belong to the universe. When you play the leaf, that sound becomes the solar system. People are alive because the universe is alive. We are not given life. Only from the human viewpoint are we given life. From God's or the Buddha's viewpoint, we are alive, period. Whether we die or live, we are eternally together with the universe."

In conversation Yokoyama often says, "Roshi said" or "In Roshi's sermon"; he is referring to Kōdō Sawaki Roshi. For two years, from 1940, Yokoyama stayed at Sōjiji in Tsurumi. At that time he apparently started to follow Kōdō Sawaki, and he became wholeheartedly devoted to the master. The spirit that earned Sawaki the nickname "Homeless Kōdō" seemed alive in his disciple.

Yokoyama's view of the universe is that it can never be understood, we can never know what it is, and when we know that fact, we can only believe in it, and that is when our faith pours forth. That faith, he said, is the faith of the universe.

His disciple Jōkō worked as an office temporary employee while following his religious practice. I asked him, "What prompted you to want to study under Roshi, and why did you come to his place?"

"When I was practicing at Antaiji, Roshi gave a talk. He explained what zazen was. When I saw him sitting in zazen, I thought that I must study under this man, so I signed up. That was all there was to it."

Hearing this I looked up again at the photograph of the Roshi in zazen posture. I had to agree! "Of course! That makes sense."

"Roshi, do you still practice zazen like that at the park?"

"I do. Once when I was sitting there an elderly woman came up to me and said: 'How realistic that manikin looks!' and reached out to touch me. I said, 'I'm doing zazen, M'am!' 'Oh my!' she responded."

Yokoyama imitated her in a falsetto voice and roared with laughter.

I had to see his zazen posture: "Roshi, please allow me to visit you again at Kaikoen tomorrow."

The following day the sky was clear again. It was Sunday, and I arrived a little after ten. A petite young woman was sitting on the spot I had previously occupied. Jōkō was also present. Introducing me to the young lady, Roshi said: "Thank you for joining us last night. This maiden princess has come from Ibaragi Prefecture. She brought me this, made by her mother," he said, showing me a cotton-padded jacket. It was black and I hadn't noticed it over his black robes. I turned to the maiden and said:

"Your mom must be a fan."

"It's a present for the Roshi's seventieth birthday. My mother wove it on her loom. I wasn't in time for Roshi's birthday, September 1. Our home is a temple of the Sōtō sect. Having a family along with a temple, my father can't live like Sodō-sama.

"My mother says: 'There is no purer monk than Sodō-sama,'" she continued.

"Lets do zazen," said Yokoyama. "I'll put on my *okesa* (Buddhist stole)."

When he spread his okesa, which he had taken from a silk-wrapped carrying bag, it was quite large. With Jōkō's help he tied it up. Positioning himself on his cushion, his posture was perfect. He seemed to enter the posture with true grace. Then he started to talk: "Zazen posture is the posture of non-thinking, non-conceptualizing. It is not the person sitting. Don't ever try to stop thoughts. Delusions are left as they are. What can we do with delusion? Can we use it for gambling at the pachinko parlor? For zazen? Let's sit for ten minutes."

Jōkō remained sitting in seiza doing zazen. The young woman next to me did the same. I stretched my spine, tucked in my chin, and in my own way became attentive. Here we go! Thinking it was all right to leave deluded thoughts as they are, I felt at ease. I thought, "Those travelers must be wondering to themselves what on Earth we are doing." Then, "I'm doing this in my own world." And, "How quiet!" And, "This is true refinement." In the meantime, ten minutes had passed.

> "Zazen is the highest and noblest posture for man. It is a breathing portrait. It is sculpture. That's why the main temple image (the Buddha) is in zazen posture."
>
> Jōkō declared, "It's a bit early, but we should start making the noodles," and the preparation began. Since it wasn't just water for tea, he had to use the large pan calling for a big fire. Roshi broke branches, stuffing them under the pan, and white smoke soon began to rise. The wind was blowing in my direction and my eyes started to smart. It took some time before the fire got going.
>
> All of a sudden a thought occurred to me. I'd heard that some of those who come to hear the leaf whistle gave the Roshi a contribution, and on such occasions he would write something quickly on a piece of paper and give it to them in return. I hadn't witnessed this elegant exchange yesterday or today, and I felt a pang of regret.
>
> From the other side of the white smoke Roshi was saying: "If you attach to your human form, you're in trouble. Whatever you do, you'll have worries, and through eternity there will be no hope of escape. If you let go of your human form, you won't need anything. You'll be like heaven and earth. Heaven and earth need nothing."
>
> The wind started blowing my way again. Smoke burned my eyes and hurt my nose.

Yokoyama did not usually lecture on Buddhism, but he gave a clear summary of his teaching in a letter written on February 28, 1977 to Masanori Yuno, the founder of the Tokyo Kendō Association.[15]

> My teacher, the late Sawaki Roshi, often made the following self-evaluation: "I am an eternally deluded person. No one is as deluded as I am. I am deluded with gold trimmings. How clear this is to me when I do zazen!"
>
> What a strange thing this zazen is. When we practice it, distracting ideas, irrelevant thoughts—in short, delusions, which ordinary people are made of, suddenly seem to feel an irresistible temptation to arise and appear at the surface. Then there is a desire to drive these thoughts away, an irresistible desire to which our complete effort is added. Those

---

[15] Kendō, the "Way of the Sword," is a martial art practiced with bamboo swords.

who don't do zazen know nothing about this. Why is it that when we practice, deluded thoughts continue to surface one after the other? The reason, which we learn from zazen, is that each one of us, from prince to beggar, is an ordinary (deluded) person. The attempt to drive these deluded thoughts away—delusion being so much nonsense (interfering with the happiness of oneself and others)—is also something brought home to us through zazen. We tentatively call this zazen that guides us in this way, "Buddha."

According to this teaching, simply the awareness that you are deluded, which comes from practicing zazen, makes you, in reality, a Buddha. It's zazen that teaches us that we too are deluded, and hence delivers us from this delusion. When we actually practice zazen and look carefully at all the deluded ideas that keep popping up, we realize how ordinary we are and how little we have to be proud of or to brag about; nothing to do other than quietly hide away. This is, after all, what we truly are.

Satori is being enlightened to the fact that we are deluded. There is then the desire, however small, to stop these deluded acts. That is how ordinary people are saved by zazen. So we realize, beyond a doubt, our ordinariness through our zazen practice, and any departure from zazen (Buddha)[16] will give rise to the inability to deal with these delusions and hence we will lose our way. We can say that the world has gone astray because it can't deal with its delusions. Going astray is transmigrating through the six realms [hell, the worlds of the hungry ghosts, beasts, fighting demons, humans and deities]. All the troubles in this world, political, economic and so forth, are created from situations in which the awareness of one's ordinariness is absent.

Sawaki Roshi said, "Those who are unaware of their ordinariness are from a religious point of view shallow and comical."

The devil—that is, illusion—when seen as the devil, can no longer exhibit its powers, and disappears of its own accord.

Shakyamuni was enlightened beyond all doubt to the fact that he was an ordinary person and became a Buddha. Then he began to live the life of a Buddha. When you realize your ordinariness, you are a Buddha, and when you are a Buddha, no matter how many distracting ideas and irrelevant thoughts appear they are no match for a Buddha and hence no

---

[16] Using a frequently employed convention in Japanese for expressing dual meanings, Yokoyama writes the character for "zazen" here and the phonetic script for "Buddha" next to it, indicating that one implies or is equal to the other.

longer remain obstacles. Delusions that no longer obstruct us are called fantasies. The Buddha way—the way of peace—is the turning of delusion into fantasies.

While the character of Zen is unity, within that unity there are many different characters. Zen is the original face of the universal life. It is the original face of the self. That is, as my teacher said, "There was no delusion in the past and there is no satori now. That is the original face of the self." Satori is not necessary when there is no delusion. That's why my teacher also said, "It's alright not to attain enlightenment, just be sure not to go astray.

If you don't go astray, original face is already there. So remain as you are, be your present self as it is."

To keep from going astray is to make delusion a fantasy. It doesn't matter how many deluded thoughts you have as long as they don't obstruct you. That is why in Zen it is said, "There was no delusion in the past and there is no satori now." In other words in zazen there are no delusion, no satori, no deluded people, and no Buddhas. And it is for that reason, because from the beginning there is no delusion, no satori, no saint, and no sinner in zazen that we have shikan taza—just sitting. Since there are no delusions in the past and no satori now, there is no need to seek Buddha and no hell to fall into. That's why we have strong expressions like, "Even if I fall into hell, it is of no account." The Great Teacher Sekitō (700–790) expressed shikan taza in the following way, "Even if I were, for example, to sink into delusion for eternity, I swear I would not seek the salvation of the saints." Is there a Buddha or a hell in shikan taza? There is only concentrated single-minded sitting. What a truly majestic expression Sekitō used to describe this.

In Buddhism, sitting with this kind of spiritual energy is called "right effort." Dōgen referred to this right effort as "nine nines are eighty-two." If, from the beginning, you make the effort necessary to obtain eighty-two from nine times nine, no matter how much delusion appears it won't become an obstacle.

The same Sekitō, expressing himself in a gentler manner referred to these teachings as follows: "The white cloud (delusion) is no obstacle to the great sky (zazen)." And Dōgen said: "The wind through the pines echoes in vain upon a deaf man's (a man of zazen) ears."

Though the wind through the pines blows in vain upon a deaf man's ears (eighty-two), it does blow. (Though delusions are limitless, I vow to put and end to them[17]) Because delusions never cease for us, our zazen practice never ends either. If we are resolved to practice zazen not only throughout this life but also through countless lives to come, we will then experience a feeling of majestic peace. . . .

In Kendō, too, it is not only the practice in the present life, but rather a resolve to practice through countless lives that will bring you a feeling of majestic peace.

To return to zazen that becomes shikan taza, "Zazen is an ordinary person as he always is becoming a Buddha." Here too one is becoming a Buddha to the degree that he advances of his own accord by actively sitting. If this weren't so, zazen too would be a painful ascetic practice. The zazen of "becoming Buddha" is called the teaching of zazen of peaceful repose. Concentrated single-minded practice is peaceful repose.

Since zazen is becoming Buddha in your ordinary state—as you are—it is not simply "the Buddha who is only the Buddha." And since it is the ordinary person becoming Buddha, it is not simply an ordinary person. While it is Buddha, it is not Buddha. The gist of this, or should I say the scope of this, is expressed in the teaching "not one not two." It is also called simply the teaching of not two. The Buddha Way is the teaching of not two.

With regard to Kendō, in Buddhist terms we would say, "Kendō is not for one and not for two. There is only complete effort, which is peaceful repose—that is satori. If Kendō is neither for one nor for two, then for what can we say it is? It is the same with zazen. Zazen is neither for Buddhas nor for ordinary people. For what can we say zazen is? Nevertheless there is something which is simply zazen. It is from this point of view that we get shikan taza, the zazen which is just sitting. In Buddhist terms we would say that Kendō too is shikan kendō—just Kendō.

My teacher said, "Don't spare any effort. People always hold back something when they make any kind of effort. When you hold something back, no matter what you are doing, your effort never amounts to anything. You are holding back when you say, 'It's no good' or 'I can't do it.'"

When you say, "This is it!" exerting the effort required to make nine times nine eighty-two, there is nothing you can't do. This is because we humans as primates are supposed to be able to exert effort beyond our normal capacity. In Buddhist terms we would say that the secret of whether one has awakened the Buddha mind is a question of whether one has the will to act. . . .

---

[17] A quote from the Four Bodhisattva Vows.

Diligent effort in Buddhism is not limited to this life. It includes the resolution to practice through countless births and deaths throughout eternity. I too must be resolved to practice in this way. If I am able to make this resolution, a feeling of transcendent peace will be the result. Because this peaceful mind and satori are the same, its not a matter of being enlightened to something, but rather the resolve to practice the Buddha Way with right effort—getting eighty-two from nine nines—throughout eternity. If I am able to make this resolution, I, myself, will become eternal. So satori, the peaceful mind, means becoming one with the eternal—the universal limitless eternal.

When nine nines are eighty-one, a restriction is imposed. When something has clear restrictions, it is limited. If in Kendō, you say, "If you reach this level, you're in good shape," you limit Kendō. And again, if you feel satisfaction because you are judged number one in Japan at a widely acclaimed meet, though this seems like quite a feat, it is, after all, limited. To free Kendō of its limits one must practice not only through this life but through eternity. If you practice in this manner, Kendō, like the limitless Buddhism, loses its limits. If it is limitless Kendō, even a child holding a bamboo sword for the first time is practicing limitless Kendō. And since zazen is eternal, limitless zazen, it is so for one who sits for the first time. It is never a limited practice bound by the stipulation that one should practice for so many years. The only satori that is effective, if we can use such a term, is the eternal limitless zazen, which is practiced and never abandoned or forsaken. All of the other activities and things that stink of satori amount to nothing. When you study Buddhism because you want to get such and such from it, or you want to become so and so, you impose a limit on it. That is not the boundless Buddha Way.

I truly hope that I am prepared to make the necessary effort and resolve to practice this limitless Buddha Way. If I were to put a limit on this practice, it would be the resolution to practice throughout eternity. Since this is the resolution of a true zazen practice, won't you make this resolution the "limit" for your Kendō practice? This is the limitless limit.

○

Monks in twentieth-century Japan were expected to reside in temples, lecturing their parishioners and teaching their disciples. Some, such as Yokoyama's teacher, Kōdō Sawaki, tried to follow the way of the ancients, wandering and living in poverty. But Yokoyama's chosen style of life was unique even when compared to the eccentric Zen teachers of old.

Though Yokoyama spoke of teaching zazen once he had fulfilled his vow to sit in Kaikoen Park for twenty years, he could no more leave the spot when two decades had passed than could the trees that surrounded him. And to the many who visited the park, the sight of Yokoyama in his seat under the sky was a more effective lesson than a thousand sermons, bringing them joy and perhaps even a glimpse of a spiritual alternative to the humdrum conformity of daily life.

2 KŌDŌ SAWAKI

THE COMMUNITY

While many Westerners came to Antaiji and left soon after, a nucleus of people stayed and maintained a zazen practice at the temple. A majority of these foreigners lived in Gentaku, the name of the neighborhood surrounding the temple. Though most of us had our own apartments and private lives, a loose community did develop. For many of us who questioned the conventional lives of the people in the worlds we left behind, it was the first time to feel some sense of being settled—a sense that came primarily from the sitting practice we shared at Antaiji. Many felt that they were doing something constructive for the first time. This group of people who previous to their arrival at Antaiji felt out of place in the world now generated considerable excitement and creative energy.

We sat the sesshins; there was no reason to be at Antaiji if you didn't. Sesshins were the core, the heart of the practice. Zazen was the hub and sesshins were the center of the hub. You felt like a bona fide member of the Zen world when you sat sesshin. It didn't matter how much your mind wandered or how much your body reeled, if you sat sesshin you were a member in good standing.

I was lucky to have sat my first three sesshins while living at Antaiji. If you lived at the temple, you were required to sit the full sesshin. I got used to sitting full sesshins before I had any choice and never allowed myself to choose otherwise when I was free to. Once I had acquired the habit of sitting, I had no desire to skip any part of sesshin. My obsession to sit every hour might even be seen as neurotic. Whatever the reason, I am grateful for having gotten into the habit. I imagine sitting must feel interminable when you know you can leave at anytime and are constantly battling with that possibility.

Uchiyama knew that many of those who lived outside of the temple had full-time jobs. If he required all to commit to sit the whole sesshin, many wouldn't be able to participate at all. His policy resulted in a zendō crowded in the evenings and on the weekends and much emptier during the week. The changing cast may have been a distraction to those who sat throughout, but since it was the result of an effort to allow as many as possible to practice, it felt right.

The zazen culture promoted at Antaiji energized us and spurred us on. It may have also deferred the feeling of smallness that I believe eventually hits all who continue sitting sesshins. You can feel pretty important after sitting a sesshin, especially when you hear all the monks calling it "the essence of Zen." The belief that you will feel something very special at some point during sesshin can keep you high with anticipation for quite a while, but when after many sesshins your expectations aren't fulfilled, you start to wonder what you are doing sitting all those hours on your black cushion. At some point (if you continue) you drop those expectations, and with them you drop that feeling of expectation, which is really no more than self-importance, too.

These intensive meditation retreats, though somewhat mechanical themselves, seem to be designed to awaken you from mechanical, unaware existence. Long and consecutive days of intensive zazen require new ways of dealing with physical and mental pain, boredom, and fear. The feeling of desperation, resulting from growing leg and back pain on the physical level and from boredom and racing thoughts on a mental level, can eventually trigger the body to overcome these physical and mental obstacles. I'm sure that similar experiences occur wherever one sits sesshins; Uchiyama, however, had a particular style that encouraged us to fall back on our own resources to deal with the personal hardships that sesshin presented. Though each Japanese Zen teacher has a personal style recognizable in sesshin, he usually stays pretty close to prescribed traditional structures. Uchiyama was unique in this respect, creating structures that were quite modern. He felt that with the exception of zazen itself, dependency on forms or on teachers was a trap that would ultimately prove harmful to his students.

The stick or kyōsaku, for example, was never used during sesshins at Antaiji. Uchiyama didn't want the distraction of someone walking in back of practitioners to disturb their zazen, nor did he want students to depend on the stick to wake them up. The stick was there, on the altar, standing idle—though I once found it useful. The zendō, like many older Japanese buildings, housed a healthy population of large centipedes—about three inches and possessing a vicious sting. When a centipede appeared near your cushion during sesshin, you were faced with a choice: getting bit or disturbing your fellow practitioners. One sesshin I found a centipede by my cushion just before the bell rang for the first sitting after lunch. There were few people in the zendō at that time, and I went up to the altar, took the stick, and crushed the centipede. When I mentioned this to the head monk apologetically at the end of sesshin, he smiled and said: "That's OK; we have to use the kyōsaku for something."

Sesshin started at four in the morning. We would pass through two big wooden doors that squeaked loudly when opened or closed and go to our cushions. Uchiyama would enter quietly, with no ceremony, and go to his cushion and sit. By 4:10 everyone was seated on their cushions and, creaking stridently, the main doors were shut as a large drum was hit to mark the official start of the first sitting. I can still call up the mixed feeling of trepidation and exhilaration that accompanied that early morning drum beat. It was the last loud noise until the sesshin's end. From that point on people entered and exited the zendō through a small sliding side door. The final sitting period of sesshin, days later, ended with the screeching sounds of the main door opening again.

The long sittings, the relative lack of ceremony, and, for some, the feeling of a lack of support sent people looking for other places to practice. But those were also the very things that kept those of us who stayed at Antaiji. We thought we were being supported without being smothered, and that suited our temperament just fine.

Everyone was welcome to stay for meals and spend the night during sesshin. The meals were simple and wonderful, cooked by Jōshin, the only resident nun at Antaiji. This little woman's devotion to feeding all participants, cooking on wood fires, carrying heavy tubs of rice, and remaining invisible whenever possible, struck me as a lesson in intelligent humility, more important perhaps than sesshin itself. Despite the fact that we had to endure the discomfort of eating rather quickly and sitting in Japanese traditional position, kneeling with your buttocks resting on your ankles, some part-timers would show up an hour before lunch, sit, go to lunch, sit another hour and leave—a tribute, I believe, to Jōshin's wonderful meals.

The meals were eaten quickly and people conducted themselves quietly, but not as quietly as at sesshins at most other Japanese temples. Bowls clacked as new people unsuccessfully tried to quietly place them on the table in front of them or to noiselessly stack them inside each other and wrap them in the formal way. As Uchiyama often said, "Quiet comes when your mind slows down enough to hear the noise." It was not uncommon for him to compare life at Antaiji with life at other Zen monasteries. "At other temples," he would say, "you are told to make sure your sandals are neatly lined up with the other sandals. At Antaiji, through your sitting practice you start to notice when things are out of order. At other temples, you are told to keep from making noise with your lacquered eating bowls. At Antaiji, through your sitting practice, you start to hear the noise and then stop creating it."

One more aspect of the sesshins that made Antaiji feel different than other temples was the lack of emphasis on the role for individual satori or kenshō. Everyone who stayed with the sesshins at some point had something that could be interpreted as a breakthrough. On the second day of my second sesshin, just when I started to wonder whether I could physically make it through the entire five days, a feeling of desperation gave way to one of comfort bordering on elation. The physical pain disappeared and I experienced a semi-euphoric state. I even remember worrying that my legs might be permanently damaged, since they no longer ached. The rest of the sesshin for me was simply enjoying this tranquil state. When I mentioned this to Lew, who had over a year of Antaiji sesshin experience at that time, he said with a sardonic smile, "Don't worry, the pain will come back." And it did. In my seven years at Antaiji that followed, I never again experienced a sesshin as physically exhilarating and as painless as that second sesshin.

When people would relate their feelings of elation during zazen to Uchiyama, wondering whether they had experienced some degree of satori, he would tell them to check the weather outside at these times—implying that the elation they experienced was simply the body's response to the good weather. Uchiyama's physical frailty may have made him particularly susceptible to changes in weather, and he may have been oversimplifying, but I also believe he was trying to help us see that these experiences of elation had mundane, rational explanations, and the quicker we accepted this the quicker we could learn what zazen really has to teach.

So what is it zazen had to teach? Five days of sitting with, in Uchiyama's words, "no toys," can get quite boring, once the pain in your legs and back subsides. We try to deal with boredom during sesshin the same way we deal with it at other times—through some kind of escape. But there aren't many escape hatches during sesshin. Whatever you do in order to escape the boredom—thinking of the next meal, planning what you will do after sesshin, and so forth—you *see* yourself doing it. You become more aware of how you operate in a state of mental discomfort such as boredom. The sesshin both intensifies our mental activities and feelings and minimizes the distractions that normally obscure them, so that inevitably we see them for what they are—a result not as exotic as I expected at the time, but infinitely more valuable in the long run.

○

Ding... ding... ding....

Bang! I wake up with a start—feels like I went to sleep about a minute ago. People all around me are folding futons, each waiting for the person before him to stuff his futon in the closet, then running outside to relieve himself and splash water on his face in order to wake up. It must be more difficult for the women in the next room, having only a few enclosed toilets. There are not nearly as many women though.

Within ten minutes the futons are all put away and everyone has dressed, entering the zendō from the main door. Some people, mostly Westerners, come directly from their homes. I bow, enter the zendō right foot first, and go to the same cushion I sat on last sesshin and will sit on next sesshin and the next, until one day I will enter the zendō and someone will be sitting on "my" cushion. I bow to my cushion, turn around, bow to the person across from me, quickly check out the zendō—Uchiyama hasn't arrived yet, and I sit.

The zendō, a large L-shaped building of approximately eight hundred square feet, is divided by a partition. The old section, the main part of the zendō—by far the oldest building in the Antaiji complex—has enough cushions and sitting space to seat all the monks. Most of the lay people, including foreigners, sit in the new section.

My mind immediately starts to race: cold this morning, straighten your back, push your chin in, drop your shoulders, Hanamura is sitting next to me again, she really sits well, looks tough....

I'm sleepy but not nodding. So many nodders; monks nodding in the very first hour. Concentrate on your own zazen, schmuck. Mind finally slowing down and the bell rings. Kinhin (walking meditation) is always a joy unless the zendō is full. Stay near the person in front of you, but not too close, halfway between the one in front and the one in back.

The 5:00 AM sitting begins. It starts to get lighter outside. Why is it that as the sun begins to rise it seems to get colder? It can't really get colder, can it? Must be some kind of physical illusion. Probably the heat from a night wrapped in my blankets accompanied me into the zendō and has now completely escaped.

We sit the second hour of sesshin. Halfway through the sitting occasional sounds of lids, utensils hitting against one another, and Jōshin, the nun who cooks, moving ever so quietly. Time passes and intervals between kitchen sounds become shorter. Perhaps it is the nervousness of sesshin and the relief offered by meals, for my stomach is already telling my brain it is hungry. Anticipation of a meal at 6:00 AM, hours before I eat breakfast on non sesshin days, grows with the increasing sounds of the kitchen. I can smell the wood burning, rice boiling, the pickles as they are being cut, and the strong odor of onions—though this is all happening on the other side of the temple complex; I can feel Jōshin's *pace picking up, her movements displaying an increasing disregard for the quiet of sesshin as she races to be ready with the miso soup and rice gruel at exactly 6:00 AM.*

All of a sudden, the morning chirping of the birds is drowned out by the sound of Jōshin clacking the clackers. First very slowly, gradually, steadily faster and faster, ending in two medium-paced clacks. The feeling of release from the tension of the early sitting, body changing, mind shifting gear. The timekeeper reaches over and rings the bell to the final clack of the clackers. The line moves into the makeshift dining hall, starting with Uchiyama, followed by the head monk, then on through to the last monk in order of their rank, after which come the lay community in order of their cushion position. Long, low tables are lined up through the room where the non-resident lay-practitioners slept, changing its use and name in typical Japanese fashion. Big tubs of rice gruel and miso soup are spaced in even intervals along the table. Uchiyama is at the head of the table, Kōhō, the head monk, is next, and the other monks and lay practitioners are arranged in the same order as in the line leading from the zendō. Kōhō watches Uchiyama, clackers in hand, while those closest to the vats prepare to serve. Kōhō takes his signal from Uchiyama's readiness, clacks the clackers, and the ceremony of serving the food in silence, using hand signals to demonstrate when you've had enough, begins. Hot rice gruel tastes good on a cold morning. But I can't eat it fast enough. It's too hot. How do those monks do it? They slurp it down, never letting it stay more than an instant in their mouths. They eat three bowls to my one.

Meal over, pour tea into a grimy bowl. Wipe it with soft pickled vegetable. Eat vegetable, drink tea. Wipe and wrap bowls. The rituals during sesshin at Antaiji are direct expressions of quiet efficiency. In less than twenty minutes thirty people are fed, bowls are cleaned, wiped and wrapped in cotton cloths, the tubs are brought into the kitchen, and the tables wiped clean. The train of participants quickly makes its way to the zendō for kinhin before the break begins.

It is early Friday morning, so the number of participants is few and things go easily and smoothly. Because sesshin has just started, however, a rhythm hasn't quite developed and I still feel a bit unfocused.

After a twenty-five minute break, we are all back in the zendō for five sitting periods that lead up to lunch. These periods, especially the last three, are my most concentrated. The small breakfast is enough to satisfy without making me feel overfull. The five periods after lunch are more distracting; the first two from eating too much, a sort of postmeridian dip, and the last three from the increasing pain in my legs. The two sittings after dinner have their own distinct quality. I realize more and more with each sesshin and the ever-repeating patterns how much the mind plays in all this. I'm tired so my mind rambles, but the pain recedes some. Just knowing there are only two more sittings allows me to loosen up, and the pain recedes as a result.

Gradually the number of lay Japanese participants and Westerners begins to grow. By Saturday evening the zendō is full and the sleeping rooms have reached capacity—we sleep shoulder to shoulder. There are always a few snorers, so sleep becomes intermittent. As one of the snorers, I feel bad about keeping others awake. I try to sleep on my side to prevent snoring, but the flat futon makes me change positions constantly as my shoulders begin to hurt. The longer I sit, the more soundly I sleep, and the problem goes away by the fourth day.

Something happens during the afternoon of the third day that happened last sesshin and the sesshin before and the one before that. Things clear up, concentration becomes easier, and though the crowd of participants grows, everyone seems to move in unison. The uniform response must be related to the fact that sesshin is half over. Though I'm not always consciously thinking about this fact, it affects me psychologically, and from now on the sesshin flies.

Sesshin is over. I enjoy the final tea party; Uchiyama greets and questions new participants and regular lay practitioners he sees only at these times. The tea party is over quickly and we are on our way. I go with some friends to a public bath. It feels wonderful. No satoris, no regrets this sesshin. I cut the after-sesshin party and go home. I don't get into parties these days; I just want to go home and enjoy this feeling of relaxation.

○

The after-sesshin parties could get pretty wild. There was beer and sake and some monks got quite drunk. Uchiyama didn't take part, but he knew what was happening and accepted it as part of temple life.

Many of the monks were young, and sesshins made them quite tense. The parties—and the alcohol in particular—allowed them some relief from the five days of intense practice. It takes time, years for some, before sesshin becomes a calming force in one's life. For monks who were at the temple for reasons quite different than those that drew the Westerners there—family pressure, failure in their studies, career security, to name a few—sesshins could be a dreaded activity that they had no choice but to bear as best they could.

But the parties were not just drinking bashes; you also had to be prepared to sing a song. Those who had a talent for singing looked forward to the opportunity to show off their voices, but for the rest of us it was a dreaded event.

The Western community had its own parties occasionally, and as the monks from Antaiji became more comfortable around us, some started showing up at the parties.

At some point our parties started featuring amateur theatricals, which become such an attraction that they drew audiences of foreigners and Japanese from all over Kyoto. People who would never travel far to see serious drama came from the other end of Kyoto to see the spectacle of gaijin making fools of themselves in these silly skits. These parties also helped us release the tensions we felt as outsiders in Japan.

Sitting sesshin did not come easy to anyone. For the Westerners, who were accustom to sitting on chairs, sitting cross-legged could be particularly painful. One Australian fellow named Greg, who arrived in Japan around the same time I did, had extreme difficulty sitting in the lotus posture. His excitement for the practice, like his excitement for most challenging endeavors, was impressive, but his physical difficulty in sitting cross-legged was compounded by a fertile mind full of projects, real and imagined.

Uchiyama was very tolerant of people coming and going in the middle of sesshin, and he never questioned those who got up and left. He even went so far as to say that if you are pursued by a recurring thought that takes over your mind and you can't drop it, it might be wise to get off your cushion and follow it through. So when Greg found himself during sesshin thinking about baking bread and he couldn't let the idea go, he got up, left the zendō, and boarded a train for Kobe, where he could buy whole-wheat flour.

He later told me that a feeling of tremendous guilt hit him the moment he left the zendō and followed him all the way to Kobe. He went to Uchiyama after sesshin and told him about the incident. Uchiyama said, "You came back, didn't you?"

Greg seemed to have energy for everything. He introduced and directed our amateur plays for the parties, made home movies, molded candles, and was always building something. When we heard of another fellow in our group sitting nine hours a day, Greg said we would all be doing that some day.

"Why would anybody want to spend the whole day sitting?" I asked.

"To stay out of trouble," was his reply.

This novel philosophy was to grow on me. Maybe zazen was learning how "not to change things." It seemed a lot closer to what Uchiyama was trying to point to than the idea of sitting to attain a state of realization. Of course to Greg, whose abundant energy pulled him every which way, it made great sense.

KŌDŌ SAWAKI ROSHI

Kōdō Sawaki, the teacher most responsible for the existence of this unusual temple, also seemed to have an abundance of energy in his youth—which sometimes got him into trouble. As he matured he found a way to constructively channel that energy and become one of the leading Japanese Zen Masters of the twentieth century.

Sawaki died in 1965, four years before my first trip to Antaiji, so I never had the opportunity to meet him; he was, however, frequently spoken of around the temple and most of the people who practiced there were greatly influenced by him. I remember Uchiyama in a lecture saying, "After spending twenty-five years studying under Sawaki Roshi, I don't know whether the words I am using are mine or his."

I once received a tape of one of Sawaki's final lectures, delivered when he moved to Antaiji at the end of his life.

O

"Kōdō Sawaki Roshi lectures on Dōgen Zenji's 'Bendōwa.' This tape was recorded in the spring of 1964 at Antaiji Temple in Kyoto." The recorded voice speaks over the somber tones of chanting.

Then a strong gruff voice takes over—it is Kōdō Sawaki in his eighty-third year.

"The 'Bendōwa' is the first chapter of the Shōbōgenzō . . ."

Sawaki explains the origin of the text, where the first copy was discovered and who found it. He talks about the meaning of the characters that make up the title "Bendōwa." "The character 'ben' means power or energy and 'dō' stands for way. So it means to put energy into the Way. The expression 'bendōwa' came from the Record of Wanshi Zenji."

After quoting Wanshi's use of the word, Sawaki equates bendō with zazen. He proceeds to read from the text. "All Buddhas together have been simply transmitting this wondrous dharma. . . . The wondrous dharma, which has been transmitted only from Buddha to Buddha without deviation, has as its criterion jijuyū samadhi."

"Jijuyū samadhi," Sawaki explains, "is 'zazen that comes to nothing.' You have to forget any results of your effort. Result-oriented practice is merely an enterprise, a business. Monks say that they have no time to do zazen."

"I always say zazen is an activity that comes to nothing" he repeats. "There is nothing more admirable than this activity that comes to nothing."

"To do something with a goal is really worthless." The inevitable Zen paradox.

These opening words give a wonderful summary of the teaching of this unique Zen personality. Though Sawaki's health was failing when he gave this lecture, his voice is clear and vibrant.

I imagine him unable to use his legs any longer and being carried down from his second-floor room at Antaiji by a few disciples. He gets behind the table, opens his text, and an explosive energy emerges from him: a "bendōwa," a putting of energy into the Way. He is a scholar—talking of the origins of the 'Bendōwa,' the influences on Dōgen when he wrote it, and Dōgen's unusual use of the Japanese and Chinese languages. He is a rebel—badmouthing the Zen institutions with their lazy clerics. But most of all, he is waving a banner for zazen—the zazen known as shikan taza, or just sitting, a zazen that he insists has absolutely no value in the sense of progress, benefits, or in, his everyday language, "paybacks." "Because it takes you out of the world of loss and gain," he says, "it should be practiced."

O

When I arrived at Antaiji in 1969 for a summer training period, I spoke no Japanese. I met an American (whose name I never caught) who had trained for some time at Antaiji. He told me that Uchiyama's teacher Sawaki Roshi was said to be the only twentieth-century Zen master who truly understood Dōgen's teaching—quite a sweeping statement for a newcomer to Japan with limited Japanese language skills to make, but since I had spent less time in Japan than he did and spoke no Japanese at all, I just accepted it.

Sawaki was a unique figure in modern Japanese Zen. He traveled the country running retreats and giving lectures. He spoke from his experiences as well as from his understanding of Buddhism, and he didn't pull his punches. One who studies the Zen of Tang China (618–906) might wonder what was so unusual about someone as outspoken as Sawaki, but the Zen world in modern-day Japan is not that of Tang China. Zen in modern Japan is part of an established religious sect in an affluent, rigidly hierarchical country. Many people have been attracted to Sawaki because of his uninhibited speech and somewhat eccentric manner. Having read so much about the artless Zen masters of old, they were excited to find someone in modern times who seemed to be following in their tradition.

It is not surprising that a temple as offbeat as Antaiji traces its beginnings to one of the most eccentric Japanese Zen personalities of the twentieth century. Kōdō Sawaki was not listed as the founding abbot of Antaiji, nor did he live there until his failing health forced him to. The honor of recognition as the temple's founder went to Sōtan Oka, one of Sawaki's teachers, famous for his Dōgen scholarship—though Oka may never have actually set foot on Antaiji soil.

Although Sawaki never settled at Antaiji until his final years when sickness and failing legs made travel impossible, the mark of his presence there was indelible. Orphaned at an early age and adopted by a family who took advantage of him rather than cared for him, he survived to become a noted Dōgen scholar, professor of Komazawa University, and the *godō* (overseer of practice) at Sōjiji. But the impression left upon those of us who learned of him while practicing at Antaiji through the stories told by his disciple Uchiyama was of a wise eccentric who traveled the country practicing zazen and Buddhism passionately and without regard to social conventions and niceties. "My father," recalled Sawaki, "was said to be good-natured, honest, and mild; my mother was a strong-minded, able woman. We were four children, but I was the only one raised solely on breast milk. That may have been the reason my physique was stronger than those of my siblings. My father pampered me a lot as a young child and never scolded me. I remember him carrying me up a small hill on clear days to watch the sunset."[1]

This idyllic life didn't last very long, though Sawaki may have derived from it the strength to endure the hardships that were to plague him through most of his childhood and adolescence. He was born Saikichi Tada in Tsu City in Mie Prefecture on June 16, 1880. His father Sōtaru had a business making metal components for rickshaws, but it wasn't sufficient to keep his determined mother from running a rice store by herself during this time.

When Saikichi was five years old his mother died. Three years later his father died and the children were distributed among the relatives, who were too poor to keep all the siblings together.

"At first they wanted to send me to a temple. But my aunt and uncle said, 'He's so mischievous he'd never settle down in a temple. What's more we have to make sure that when he grows up he doesn't come back to us with a vendetta for sending him to a temple.' And they decided against it. They eventually sent me to my aunt on my father's side."

After a short period with his aunt and her husband, who beat Saikichi every time his spoiled four-year-old cousin Matsu decided to cry and blame his misfortune on Saikichi, he was again left parentless. When this stepfather who "fed me leftovers while serving his precious Matsu delicacies" died suddenly, he left Saikichi without anyone to care for him, and the boy realized how important his guardian had been, even if he treated him badly. "Even the little rascal I was" he remarked years later about his feelings of desperation "went down for the count."

Saikichi was finally passed on to an associate of a distant relative, a maker of lanterns named Bunkichi—who was also a professional gambler and in Sawaki's words a "cheater of cheats." His new mother, Bunkichi's eleventh wife, was a veteran prostitute subject to severe fits of hysteria. Bunkichi and his wife treasured young Saikichi for the liveliness he brought to their home—and the fact that they could put him to work while they drank and gambled the days away.

Sawaki recalled an incident in which he learned not to lie, along with an additional lesson on impermanence. At the age of nine he was walking by a prostitute's

---

[1] This and all subsequent quotes about Sawaki's life, unless otherwise noted, were taken from *Kōdō Sawaki Kikigaki* (Tokyo: Kōdansha, 1984).

quarters and saw a group of people gathered at the door. Having played hide-and-seek there many times before, he was quite comfortable going up to the second floor where the bedrooms were. There he saw the corpse of a man about fifty years old, a young prostitute around seventeen or eighteen in her night clothes sitting by the bed with a disinterested look on her face, and a woman who appeared to be the dead man's widow crying by his side. "Even in death you are a disappointment," she was lamenting, "Why in this place? And for all the world to see." This incident led Sawaki to philosophize:

> I realized then that people can't depend on keeping anything secret. And that's not all. His poor widow would be dishonored with each memorial service, when she and others would be reminded that the 'dear departed' had died in the bedroom of a young prostitute on the second floor of a whorehouse.
>
> There are many ways to contemplate impermanence. As a young child I lost my mother and my father; my uncle collapsed in front of me and was dead within seconds. Still, I did not become keenly aware of impermanence. At those times I just worried about who would raise me in the future.
>
> Dōgen lost his mother when he was eight years old; it is said that seeing the smoke from the funeral incense rising awakened a sense of impermanence in him. People of lower realms like myself don't have that kind of experience. However, having vividly experienced sudden deaths and finally, on top of that, this one, I couldn't help but feel the reality of impermanence to the marrow of my bones. This time, even one as dull as I couldn't avoid the heartfelt contemplation of impermanence.
>
> I experienced impermanence in this manner because of the environment in which I lived. The place where I was raised was the worst, the lowest of the low. There was absolutely no encouragement whatsoever to build character or to learn. But for that very reason it turned out to be the best learning environment of all.

Sawaki goes on to describe his neighborhood, with its prostitutes, pimps, and pickpockets, and how by nine or ten he became familiar with this world and knew everything that was going on and why:

> This was the environment in which I was raised. I guess you could call it living on the fringes of society. Had I been fully immersed in it, I wouldn't have felt its inherent contradictions, but in fact while living in this world

as a child of nine or ten, there was someone who was teaching me about another world outside a world of money, food, pleasure and titles, a world in which people live worthy lives.

Sawaki is referring to the house of a friend, Morita Senshū, the son of the owner of a framing and papering business. Senshū was six years older than the young Sawaki, and it was at his house that Sawaki first heard about the history and literature of China and Japan and was infused with a love of learning. He learned about artists who lived near the poverty level but never concerned themselves about money or titles. Sawaki remained impressed with the beauty and the sense of values of this new world—so different from those of his youthful milieu—for the rest of his life: "When I went to Senshū's house, I felt an atmosphere of purity that radiated from the whole family, and, at some point, I felt 'I want to be a seeker of the Way.'"

Sawaki's friend Senshū died a poor man. He lived a simple life, running his family business and painting. It was Senshū's simplicity, his learning, and his lack of desire for money or fame that impressed Sawaki and gave direction to his life.

Sawaki continued living with his adopted parents, selling pounded rice cakes to help support them while they gambled and drank their lives away. Along with the influence of Senshū and his family, visits to a nearby Jōdo Shin (True Pure Land) temple inspired him with hope for the future. One story that impressed him deeply was that of the young ascetic Sessen Dōji, a previous incarnation of the Buddha. While Sessen was practicing in the Himalayas, the deity Shakra decided to test him, disguising himself as the demon Rakshasa, and reciting the first half of a verse, "All things are impermanent / They appear and disappear." Sessen, elated upon hearing the first half of the verse, said he would become the demon's disciple if he could hear the rest of it. When the demon claimed he was so hungry he couldn't remember the second half, Sessen offered his body as food if he were allowed to hear it. Then the demon recited, "Put an end to appearance and disappearance / Nirvana is realized." Sessen proceeded to write these lines on rocks, trees, and paths, and then was about to throw his body from a tall tree to offer himself as food for the demon when Shakra changed back to his real form and saved the boy.

Hearing this story as a boy, Sawaki only understood that a boy was willing to throw away his body to hear the Dharma, but that was enough. Other stories about the nobility of becoming a monk and devoting one's life to seeing the Way roused in Sawaki a desire to leave his present situation and do the same. He had run away from home once before, but this time his resolve was stronger: "I kept thinking, 'I want to be a monk, I want to be a monk.' I didn't care if I died in the process."

Sawaki went to the Shin priest whose sermons had made such a great impression on him and spoke of his intention to become a monk. "If you want to be a monk," the priest said, "don't get married. I have five children and my wife is dead. I have my hands full with my own children and could never care for another. Unmarried Shin Buddhist priests are criticized for having a wrong understanding of Buddhism. Don't become a Shin Buddhist priest. Zen monks aren't expected to have wives; you should become a Zen monk."

Sawaki immediately set out for Eiheiji: "I didn't have any particular reason to choose Eiheiji," he recalled, "other than that it was far enough away so they wouldn't easily be able to bring me back, and because the Shin priest advised me to become a Zen monk." Sawaki set off with a lantern, and the clothes on his back. On his way out of town he visited the Shin priest who had recommended he become a Zen monk. The priest gave him three and one-half liters of rice and a small amount of money to help him on his journey, which he spent on ferry fares, stamps to send cards informing his family of his decision to leave home for good, and roasted soybeans to eat on the way.

After four days on ferries and on foot, spending nights in small shrines built for religious pilgrims, he arrived at Eiheiji. His joy was quickly tempered when he was refused entry to the monastery.

> Finally, I arrived at Eiheiji, explained my situation and asked to be allowed to be ordained, but they clearly weren't going to accept me. I was told unconditionally to go home, my plea falling on deaf ears. "I can't go back home," I said, "I'm famished, I can't move. Let me die here."
>
> "We'll let you have some leftover rice gruel. Go home as soon as you've finished," was the response I got.
>
> "Then," I said, "don't bother feeding me." And I continued making my plea for two days and nights without eating or drinking. Finally a priest named Jikizō, the person in charge of building and repairs, observed my condition and couldn't remain indifferent. He asked me to come to his place and invited me in. Letting me stay in the worker's room with the menservants for the time being, he managed to get me into the temple.
>
> I will never in my life forget the feeling of joy I had when, after all I had endured, I was allowed to stay with the menservants! I couldn't help shedding tears of gratitude, and each and every monk I met appeared to me to be a bodhisattva.
>
> At that time, I was wearing an unlined, striped kimono, my only clothes. The master of the Hakuju Hermitage, a hermitage in front of

> Eiheiji's main gate, gathered torn robes thrown away by practitioners, and sewing them together, made monk's robes for me. He put them on me and I somehow looked like a monk. I was so moved and joyful that tears streamed down my face.

Sawaki stayed on with the workers for a while, but he wasn't allowed to be ordained. He had to find a teacher in some other temple who would accept him as a disciple. He went to other temples only to be used by lazy priests looking for disciples to legitimize their positions and relieve them of part of their own workload. Frustrated, he returned to Eiheiji, where he was befriended by a monk named Kōun Yamamoto. Kōun recognized Sawaki's seriousness and recommended he go to Japan's westernmost island of Kyūshū and study with Kōun's teacher Kōhō Sawada.

Sawaki set out for Kumamoto Prefecture with no money or supplies. His battered monk's robes allowed him to spend nights at temples on the way, and he was usually sent off the next day with a box lunch. The trip was arduous, leading through mountain passes in midwinter, and he suffered from severe frostbite of the feet, among other things. At that point he realized he couldn't continue on to Kyūshū, and he took refuge in his sister Sai's home in Ueno in Iga Province. She was the wife of the proprietor of a fish shop. Sai attended to his injuries, but only after taking him outside and stripping all his clothes off. Sawaki was full of lice. He realized that there must have been quite a commotion when he left those temples where he'd spent nights between Eiheiji and his sister's home, and he felt terrible.

His brother-in-law, seeing him in tattered robes, lice-ridden, and frostbitten, tried to persuade him to give up his dream of being a monk and settle with them as a fishmonger. Sawaki thanked him but, when his wounds healed, he set out once again for Kyushu. The rest of the trip didn't go much better: "I boarded a ferry near Kobe. There was a big fuss when one of the passengers lost three yen. Being the most ragged-looking passenger, I was suspect. 'I would never do anything wrong,' I protested, 'I am on my way to Kyushu from Eiheiji for religious practice. I am poor but I wouldn't steal even if my life depended on it.' No one believed me."

Sawaki was put in jail for a month. He learned about life in prison, which was to help him many years later when he was asked to give sermons to prisoners. During his incarceration, the other prisoners laughed at him when they found out he was in jail for something as minor as stealing—and they laughed even louder when he denied doing it.

After being released he continued on to Kyushu. He arrived at Kōhō Sawada's temple, Shōshinji, eleven months after leaving Eiheiji, on December 8, 1897. He was eighteen years old.

SEEDS OF A GROWING FAITH IN THE ZAZEN POSTURE

Sawaki and his disciple Sodō Yokoyama talked much about the zazen posture, elevating the posture itself to a transcendental status; as though the posture will dissolve your delusions if you just allow it. An incident at Shōshinji was to help plant the seed for such a view of zazen in the young Sawaki.

> At the temple at Amakusa, everyone got up at four in the morning. I used to rise before that and do zazen by myself. I was once left to watch the temple when everyone had gone out. Perfect, I thought, and went to the *hondō*, the main temple building, to do zazen. At that time, the old lady who cooked at the temple probably thought that the novice who had just arrived and was supposed to be watching the temple was surely taking it easy, maybe even sleeping, so she decided to drop into the hondō. Surprised to find me sitting by myself, upright in zazen, she dropped to the floor, bowing with hands folded; she bowed a hundred times more than she'd ever bowed to the Buddha.
>
> This old lady, who usually mocked me, the new arrival, by calling me *kozō* (temple errand boy) and working me to the bone, bowed to the form of zazen with greater care than she usually gave to the Buddha. This started me pondering deeply. I realized that zazen is a very remarkable thing.

He went on to talk about the way we generally calculate greatness by measurable achievements. Zazen, however, he said, as shown in the incident with the old cook, was instantly recognized and bowed to without measure or calculation. The posture, he said, is the Buddha; it is not delusion. This was his firm conviction from then on.

Sawada taught Sawaki how to read sutras in a powerful, full-throated voice. He also gave Sawaki the Buddhist name Kōdō as part of his official ordination. As was the practice then, once a monk learned the fundamentals of Zen monastic life he was sent out to travel a kind of "Zen circuit" in search of the Way and of a teacher to guide him in his practice. Sawaki was at that time a peculiar mixture of a diligent practitioner and a rascal, pulling pranks on monks when he sensed any pious hypocrisy or false religiosity. Young and brazen, he was an annoyance to priests, who valued proper decorum highly.

Sawaki began to practice at Entsūji, a temple in Hyōgo Prefecture, when he was twenty years old. When Ryōunji, a temple in nearby Tajima, requested the use of two monks from Entsūji to help them conduct a precepts ceremony, the head priest gladly sent the rambunctious Sawaki to get him out of the way. Sawaki was disgusted with the lack of sincerity at Entsūji and felt no great connection with the head priest, so he was only too happy to leave. Sawaki and the head priest of Ryōunji, Ryuun Fueoka, hit it off well from the start, leading Sawaki to say later that Fueoka was one of the greatest influences in his life.

Sawaki describes Ryuun Fueoka as able to move mountains with his quiet, unassuming presence. He was, for the fiery young Sawaki, a still pool, an embodiment of the principles expounded by Dōgen. Like Sawaki's neighbor and friend from the slums, the artist Morita Senshū, Fueoka had the ability to control his impulses in a way that Sawaki never could, an ability he both envied and respected. Sawaki was only able to study with Fueoka during this twentieth year; the following year, he was drafted into the army. Still, he attributes his understanding of zazen and of the need to accompany it with a thorough study of Buddhist texts to this one man. Fueoka warned Sawaki not to take a narrow view of the Zen dictum "outside the scriptures and not through words." It was primarily a result of Fueoka's influence, he said, that he decided some eight years later, to enter Hōryūji, in Nara, to study the Yogacara or Mind Only philosophy of Buddhism.

Sawaki was drafted into the army in 1900 for a three-year term of duty, after which he looked forward to returning to his Buddhist practice. Events, however, went against his plans:

> I was taken unwillingly from the Buddha Way for three years. It couldn't be helped. I had to accept it as one would a natural disaster. When my term was up, I thought to myself, 'This time I will practice fully.' Just then we were informed of the start of the Russo-Japanese War and I was given an order to report back for duty upon completion of the previous duty period. It was a real setback to my keen aspiration to practice the Way. For the first and last time in my life I composed a poem: 'I thought to devote this body to the Way / I end up a country-defending devil!'

Sawaki discussed his military experiences in detail, pointing out (just as he did about civilian life) its inherent inconsistencies, hypocrisies, and discrimination. He criticized the military leaders who acted tough in times of peace but showed their true colors, their cowardliness, when they faced actual combat. Their actions, he said, were not much different from those of the gangsters in the neighborhood in which he was reared, who acted tough until actually confronting rivals from neighboring territories—at which time they "swung their swords and knives with their eyes closed."

Sawaki's description of his own part in the fighting at the front lines has earned him the praise of many naive Japanese followers and, more recently, the blame of others, even the suggestion that he was one of the early perpetrators of an ethic that identified Zen with war. Sawaki was a survivor who grew up in a neighborhood where violence was the rule rather than the exception. He was strong and daring, and those qualities helped him survive. He was clearly not a pacifist, but neither was he a promoter of a militaristic Zen—at least not before the early 1940s, when he was living in a country under siege. Given his situation, I find it difficult to judge his actions, but the general message of his teaching was anything but that of a promoter of war.

In 1905, Sawaki was wounded, shot in the back of the neck, the bullet exiting through his mouth and taking part of his tongue with it. He was then tagged along with other wounded soldiers and placed on a mat in a field hospital: "The wounded around me were carried away [dead] and new wounded were put in their places, only to be carried off the next day. I was the only one who remained. On the third day I was still alive. Then [they thought], "We may be able to save this guy," and someone finally began to administer to my wound."

In September of 1905, Sawaki was taken back to Japan and sent to Hiroshima Hospital where he finally received professional medical care. From there he was sent to Nagoya Hospital, treated for two months, and then sent to the home of his stepparents.

> By November my wound had healed considerably and I was allowed to go home to convalesce. I initially returned to my hometown to rest and recuperate. There, after a long absence, I went to the home of my stepparents. I opened the door and stood there in a state of shock. My stepmother was there, hair disheveled, kimono untied and open, and she was smeared in her own feces and tied up. Still, when she noticed me, she called out, "Wah!" and clung to me. Though things rarely startle me, an eerie feeling ran through me. My stepmother had gone mad.
>
> My stepfather was not there. I could do nothing so I went and inquired in the neighborhood. I learned that he was gambling and had been for two or three days. I went to the pharmacy where I used to relax and was having lunch when my stepfather came in. His sleeves were rolled up and he was quite angry and was shouting: "Mom's gone crazy and business is bad, so now you have to somehow take care of me. You can't run around doing as you please like you've been doing as a monk up to now."

According to Sawaki, his stepfather was depending on his death in battle so the family could receive a hardship allowance from the government. He had borrowed money to drink, gamble, and party and spent it all. Having used up all that money and seeing his stepson return alive, he got quite angry. Sawaki borrowed money from his brother, gave it to his stepfather, and left home.

Sawaki was befriended by a Sōtō Zen monk who, like himself, had been wounded in the war. This monk let Sawaki stay at his temple for three months. When Sawaki had recovered his health, he was sent back to China as an infantryman. In 1906, he returned to Japan and was discharged from army duty.

To Sawaki, his near fatal wound that required constant care and the debt he incurred for his stepparents, which reduced him to poverty, were minor inconveniences when compared to his feeling of being far behind other monks his age in his Buddhist studies: "At that time my studies occupied me through the night. I slept soundly in the morning from five to eight. I'd get up at eight, pack a lunch from the leftovers of the night before, dilute the remainder in water, gulp it down and run [to school]. . . . I was primarily studying the Consciousness Only (Yogacara) school. It prepared me for my later studies at Hōryūji's Kangakuin."

It was around this time that Sawaki realized something about himself that was crucial to his understanding of Buddhism. He had always thought of himself as brave, having fought for survival in a tough neighborhood and risked his life on the battlefield, sometimes to the amazement of his fellow soldiers. But when an explosion in Osaka shook Sawaki's room, he was startled. As he contemplated the fear that seized him, he realized that the self-image of fearlessness that he had cherished up to then was a mere delusion: "My standing firm in the midst of war, I understood, was a result of a rush of blood to my head when I competed with others; it was nothing more than a result of a competitive spirit. I realized that I was not demonstrating true courage."

He went on to say that practicing zazen and studying the teaching of Zen Master Dōgen showed him that his so called bravery in war was a cheap, paltry thing, and as a disciple of the Buddha he was, upon reflection, quite ashamed of himself. He referred to that Sawaki as the one who "was famous for risking his life, being fearless in war, always running around stirring things up" and "the person inside the first half of my life." The present Sawaki, by contrast, was a person who "nervously let down [his] defenses" and "meekly knelt down before Zen Master Dōgen." Then he quoted from Dōgen's *Gakudō Yōjin Shū* (Points to Watch in Buddhist Training):

> Breaking one's bones and crushing the marrow appear to be difficult, but putting the mind in order is far more difficult. Prolonged austerities and pure training are also difficult, but putting your body in order is more difficult still. If one says that smashing bones was a practice to be valued, then why have so few of the many ancients who are said to have endured

those activities been enlightened? If austerities and practices are to be valued, then why have so few of the many ancients who have done them been enlightened? This is because of the extreme difficulty of putting the mind in order. Don't put brilliance of learning first. Nor should you put the conscious mind, thought, or insight first. The Buddha Way is entered when you put your mind and body in order. All those other things are useless.

Sawaki continues: "Because I entered Dōgen's school, I was able to practice [correctly]. Being a man of immoderate ways, if I hadn't followed Dōgen, my natural cunning would probably have caused me to be quite unscrupulous in business or in whatever work I pursued. Being easily angered, I might have killed somebody.

"However, I gave up [that kind of behavior] completely, acted with circumspection, and remained inconspicuous and was able to find sanctuary in a zazen that hasn't a shred of a reward. This was all thanks to Dōgen."

Here is the seed from which Sawaki's life's work came. It was not so much the uniqueness of "no-gain" zazen as it was the uncompromising stress he gave it. He drove this "zazen comes to nothing" point home so strongly that it did not appear to be a kind of Zen code for something he actually believed to be highly rewarding. After fighting his way out of the slums and believing he had to win all the time, he must have felt as though the world were lifted from his shoulders when he finally experienced letting all that go and being *nothing*.

But the seed didn't immediately become a flower. Sawaki's Hōryūji study period was just beginning. He described his "greed for Buddhist studies" as not unlike a miser's obsession with money. He ate and slept a bare minimum and his robes looked more like rags than clothing. At age thirty, he said, people mistook him for a seventy-year old man and remarked at how healthy he seemed for his advanced age.

Sawaki's competitive nature never allowed him to rest. He was determined to keep up with monks who had been successful students all their lives. He had no real background in Buddhist scholarship and had to study twice as hard to keep up with all his classmates. Upon reflection he said, "It was like I was competing for the sake of competing. It wasn't really study, it was competition." He would study so hard that he'd forget about eating and sleeping. He also loved to argue points of doctrine with students of other sects, teasing them when they didn't know a point about their own school's doctrine that he could proudly point out to them. This period, too, Sawaki looks back on with embarrassment. After reading somewhere, "There are people who forget to eat and sleep in order to study, but rarely anyone who forgets to eat and sleep for religious practice," his pride turned to shame.

As with his awakening through Dōgen's words in *Points to Watch in Buddhist Training*, he was reminded once again of the difficulty and value of calmly and clearly devoting one's life to practice. He saw his ability to make sacrifices in order to compete in studies as nothing more than the equivalent to sacrificing for name and fame.

Sawaki was a dynamic, no-nonsense individual, but difficult to classify beyond that. "Sawaki Zen" is hard to pin down, and no doubt each of his followers would describe it differently. They would all agree, however, that Sawaki believed zazen was the key to understanding Buddhism. He was an impassioned advocate of zazen. He was also a talented storyteller. He had the ability to bring the lowly circumstances of his youth to life for his audience with wit and cleverness. He was a charismatic person, but according to his disciple Uchiyama this was not always a good thing. Uchiyama felt that many people were so impressed with Sawaki's strong presence that they missed the importance of his message. Sawaki could also be crude and self-aggrandizing in his modes of expression, which at times obscured his central message of a Zen practice utterly lacking in any thought of gain or achievement.

Sawaki's studies at Hōryūji in Nara gave him a solid background for immersing himself, in his characteristic way, in the works of Dōgen. He was aided on this path by his relationship with the renowned Sōtō priest and Dōgen scholar Sōtan Oka Roshi of Daijiji. Sawaki talked about learning the fine points of Sōtō practice, such as the proper way to practice walking meditation, from Sōtan, but it was the power and the authority that his teacher's words and deeds conveyed that left the deepest mark on Sawaki. One incident, in particular, stood out in his mind. Sawaki was sitting near the interview room during sesshin, where he could hear the interview between Sōtan and a monk.

"Well, what do you want?" Sōtan's voice had such power, Sawaki said, that the monk's voice was reduced to a whisper.

"I want to understand the Great Matter please."

"Whose Great Matter?" was the teacher's brusque response.

"Um, mine..."

"What? Yours? If it's just you alone, what does it matter?" Sōtan responded with a laugh that penetrated to the pit of Sawaki's stomach, though he wasn't even in the room.

Sōtan's responses to self-centered monks who came to him with paradoxical statements that were clearly from the intellect and of no practical use, impressed Sawaki and helped him form his own approach to Zen. He grew to distrust practices that he felt could easily be reduced to mind games, and his faith in just sitting, a zazen of complete surrender in which no fruits of practice could be expected, blossomed.

Around this time Sawaki became assistant head of training at Yōsenji, a temple in Matsusaka in Aichi Prefecture. He was thirty-three years old. There Sawaki met another "champion of zazen," Kōzan Katō. The two formed an immediate friendship and were to remain close until Sawaki's death some fifty years later. Both men were looking for a place where they could practice Zen in a rigorous and serious manner and were unhappy with the lack of seriousness at Yōsenji. Neither of them stayed there very long.

After looking around for a place to continue his practice and meeting one dead end after another, Sawaki turned to his former teacher at Hōryūji, Jōin Saeki. Saeki allowed him to stay at a small temple in Nara nominally under Saeki's charge. Nobody lived in Jōfukuji when Sawaki moved in and nobody seemed to be interested in the temple or its goings on. Sawaki saw it as an opportunity to close the doors and practice uninterrupted zazen alone.

> This temple was completely veiled from society. In the three years I was there no one came to visit, which was most suitable to me. I decided to devote myself completely to zazen . . . even if I died in the process.
>
> Feeling no need to make contact with the world, I closed the gate and sat day after day, from two in the morning until ten at night: my uninterrupted sesshin had begun. . . . Days passed and nobody came to visit. I sat alone, living like this continuously for three years. As I practiced in this manner, the days and months felt long. People may think that when you practice alone, doing zazen all the time, everything will go blank, but it doesn't. The more you are alone, the more you eliminate things to do, the more things float [to the surface] like a crab blowing bubbles.

Three years of solitary zazen at Jōfukuji helped Sawaki clarify the practice of zazen, for which he had developed a deep faith. This zazen, which needed no confirmation from the outside world, was the only real zazen. He emphasized this point whenever he had the chance. Because his zazen was getting him nowhere, one monk recommended he try another field of study.

> When I was studying at Hōryūji, a friend often said to me, "Sawaki, you're always talking zazen, zazen, but you won't find people today who will listen to that kind of talk. You are going to pass your life in misery. You won't even find one person who will follow you and you will live a lonely life. Let me tell you something that won't hurt you to know. You would be better off learning English."

His prediction was on target with regard to my life at Jōfukuji. I was practicing like a freshwater clam sucking in seawater, like a parrot attempting to put out a forest fire by soaking its wings and flying through the trees. I had a vow and I believed I could not let it go unfulfilled. I believed that fulfilling this vow was nothing less than the name of all the Buddhas.

Sawaki's stories about this period of his life tell of a growing faith in zazen and of getting into various kinds of trouble—predicaments that often appeared incompatible with one who was developing strong religious faith. He told of getting sick the night before he was supposed to attend a lecture at Eiheiji because he entered an eating contest, consuming twenty-three bowls of rice with bamboo shoots and nineteen bowls of miso soup. He ended up being sent home by his teacher before the lecture, and he was quite embarrassed. Obvioulsy, his competitive nature did not drop away all at once; as he stopped competing in mundane pursuits, he seemed to get caught up competing in the realm of the absurd.

Sawaki had given up on finding people to practice with the intensity he thought necessary for one to really understand Dōgen's way, which is why he decided to sit by himself at Jōfukuji, until, as he put it, he died. But his former teacher Sōtan Oka had been asked to go to Kumamoto to Daijiji to revive this old head temple of the Sōtō sect, and Sōtan cajoled Sawaki into going there in his stead. He gave Sawaki the impression that it would be for about six months, but when, half a year later, Sawaki was ready to leave, Sōtan pleaded with him to stay on. Sawaki ended up at Daijiji until Sōtan's death some six years later. His solitary zazen was over, but he was fortunate to find students in Kumamoto who possessed the energy to practice—just the kind of practitioners he had given up searching for when he entered Jōfukuji alone three years before.

At this time Sawaki talked about being offered *junshike no inka*. In Rinzai Zen, the word *inka*, which is known as "certification" in American Zen circles, is used by a Zen master to indicate that his disciple has attained enlightenment. In orthodox Sōtō Zen there is an official transmission of the teaching, but it is not ordinarily considered a certification of enlightenment. Sawaki turned this honor down. He said that had he accepted it, he would no longer have been a free agent, traveling around the country and teaching where he pleased, and would instead be drawn inescapably into the politics of the Sōtō sect. He regarded *inka* as proof of membership in a club, and though it would have qualified him to be the next abbot of Daijiji upon Sōtan's death, he despised the whole system of Zen institutionalism and the contradictions inherent in it.

At Daijiji Sawaki found the kind of practitioners who renewed his faith in the possibility that Buddhist practice (which meant zazen to Sawaki) would return to Japan. Most of the serious students that gave Sawaki new hope in forming a real Zen community were from the Fifth Higher School. He established a rigorous schedule. Daijiji monks rose at 2:00 AM, did zazen until 6:00 AM, followed by sutra reading, breakfast, and cleaning. From 8:00 to 9:30 Sawaki lectured on Buddhism. At 11:00 the monks went out begging, and from 1:00 to 2:00 they practiced Buddhist chanting and studied Buddhist regulations. For the rest of the day, they cared for the temple grounds—mainly weeding—until nightfall. They had a late dinner and then went to bed. Sawaki stayed up until 11:00 or 12:00 PM studying before retiring for two or three hours of sleep.

Sesshins were so demanding that one wonders about their purpose. They were held monthly, each lasting five days. The schedule started as on normal days at 2:00 AM, and the sitting went on until midnight. Participants did thirty minutes of walking meditation after each meal. From midnight to 2:00 PM and from 4:00 to 5:00 PM they did zazen without the use of the kyōsaku stick (a practice known as *mensaku*). In other words, they did not lie down for the entire five days, and their only opportunity for sleep was in the seated posture, during the three hours of mensaku.

Though Sawaki seems to have found fellow practitioners whose seriousness matched his own, some parishioners had a different view of what a temple should be. They wanted a place where they could go to socialize and perhaps have a drink with the priest. When Sōtan Oka died in 1922, this group of parishioners, looking for an excuse to get rid of Sawaki, refused his proposal to make Kishizawa Ian the new abbot of Daijiji and to keep Sawaki as resident teacher. Kishizawa was in Sōtan's line and would have found no difficulty keeping Sawaki there if he were chosen as new abbot. Sawaki left Daijiji when his proposal was rejected and moved to a small house in Kumamoto lent to him by a friend.

SAWAKI AND THE FIFTH HIGHER SCHOOL STUDENTS AT DAIJIJI

Later to become the University of Kumamoto, the Fifth Higher School was reputed to be one of the best schools in the country. Its students, some of the elite of the country, were the hope of Japan's future. They were a proud bunch who thought of themselves as their country's future leaders, and their pride was accompanied by some degree of arrogance. They had a desire to learn and an abundance of energy, two qualities that appealed to Sawaki. He had a difficult time handling lethargy in his students, but he was always willing to take on arrogance.

The students of the Fifth Higher School, self-assured in their privileged status, walked around Kumamoto as if they owned the world. To some they may have seemed arrogant and spoiled, but Sawaki seems to have regarded their excess energy as a potential means of reviving Buddhism. He was asked by their principal to come to school and lecture them. The result was a relationship that Sawaki later said had a most profound effect on his life as a Buddhist priest. They questioned him about Buddhism and zazen in a manner that defied pat answers. They saw through teachers who hid behind doctrine, and they made Sawaki let go of his own preconceptions and truly open up. Nothing short of that satisfied them. They were rambunctious and played hard, but they also practiced hard. They recognized in Sawaki someone who was direct with them, and they respected him for it.

> Some Fifth Higher School students came to me one day and asked, "Oshō (Head Priest), why do you do zazen?"
> "Zazen is of no use. I just do it."
> They were surprised at my answer and I wondered whether it would have an effect on them.
> "What a candid priest! The minister never talks that way." Grumbling in this way they returned home. Then one day they appeared again.
> "Oshō, we've come to join you in something of no use."
> From then on they practiced zazen.

Though Sawaki's life as a priest was in some respects just beginning, he had already formed an approach to zazen that was to be his trademark. From this point on, he was preaching and practicing zazen wherever he could, and little by little, he became known throughout Japan as the most articulate advocate of zazen. After a year in "Daitetsudō," the name he gave his small house in Kumamoto, lack of funds made it difficult for him to continue there. Hearing of Sawaki's situation, a wealthy man by the name of Shibata, who one day had been taken by Sawaki's chanting voice, offered him his country home. The home was in a citrus orchard on top of Mount Mannichi. Shibata saw to it that Sawaki's meals were taken care of and the house became his home base as he traveled around the country lecturing and holding sesshins. For the next thirteen years Sawaki ran his "moving monastery" while living at Mount Mannichi. Over those years his reputation grew.

In 1935, he was asked to lecture on Zen literature and lead meditation practice at Komazawa University, and was appointed overseer of practice at Sōjiji. In 1940, Sawaki left Sōjiji and established Tengyō Zen'en at Daichuji in Tochigi Prefecture. It was there that he ordained Uchiyama in 1941. In 1949 Sawaki established the Shichikurin Dōjō at Antaiji. When in 1963 his aged legs and decrepit old body would no longer allow him to follow his "homeless" ways, he settled at Antaiji where he died two years later.

○

The story of Sawaki's life would not be complete without some quotes from his writings interpretating the meaning of zazen and Buddhism.

> Everyone is originally pure, not in the slightest way different from the Buddha. Zazen is the purity of one's own nature through the body. So the self of zazen is different from the self of ordinary life. With the ordinary self you are always using your mind to figure things out: how to get through this world in a better fashion, how to make money, how to move up in the world, how to make life easier, how to make it more pleasurable, how to know what is delicious and what is tasteless. Zazen puts all that aside. In other words, it takes a break from the human world. What is the human world? The five desires and the six dusts. Wanting money, wanting to eat tasty food, and wanting things to be easy. [People] spend their whole lives [seeking] sex, food, position, and the like. In zazen, however, you let go of all relationships, take a pause from everything. Don't think in terms of good or bad, or judge right from wrong. Stop the movement of consciousness. Refrain from the calculation of ideas. Don't seek to be a Buddha because that too is a desire.[2]
>
> How stupid it is for us to live in this five-foot body for fifty or eighty years! We endure throughout all eternity—we continue to live in the entire universe, for twenty-five billion years, not anything so insignificant as fifty or a hundred years. We continue to live in the great, infinite, abundant universe. The way to live in this abundant universe is through the direct [transmission] of zazen from the Buddha. That is the transmission from person to person through the mind of the mind-seal.[3]
>
> The universe and I are of the same root. The myriad things and I are one body. That is zazen.[4]
>
> If you sit with faith in zazen, you will be Buddha.[5]

---

[2] Sawaki Kodō, *Zenshū* (Collected Works), vol. 15 (Tokyo: Daihōrinkaku, 1966), 161.

[3] Ibid., 169.

[4] Ibid., 183.

[5] Ibid., 184.

We stop the one who can't cease from seeking things outside, and practice with our bodies with a posture that seeks absolutely nothing. This is zazen.[6]

Though it is thought that zazen and faith are different and said that zazen is not [related] to faith, doing zazen in this way, becoming intimate with the self, creating a very clear self, is what I call faith.

If you sit in a fog, you and zazen are two [separate things]. You don't become one with zazen; you and zazen, you and the Buddha are two. You see the Buddha somewhere far away. This is a mistake.

I believe that zazen and Sawaki are one. Zazen is Sawaki and Sawaki is zazen. However, it's not that simple. [In fact] Zazen and Sawaki are far away. I practice zazen and think about something [like] the girl I saw on the road.

Zazen soars majestically like Mount Fuji. Sit flaccidly or doze and you're not doing zazen. When I sit steadfast, zazen and Sawaki become one. That is samadhi. Samadhi is the purity of human nature. It is the true me.

The Great Priest Hakuin said: "To be absorbed in this pure human nature, you must practice zazen diligently without slacking at all."

Once years ago, in an attempt not to waste my time, I decided to make paper string as a side business. The Sawaki who spent all his time practicing zazen was defeated. Zazen defeated Sawaki. Because this zazen defeated a deluded person, my view [of zazen] was a mistaken one. I was being pulled around by zazen. A pattern was woven between zazen and me. When I practiced zazen, the pattern between us [zazen and Sawaki, or the practitioner and the practice] became evident.[7]

All the sutras are theses on zazen. . . . That's what I mean by the expression, "become intimate with the self." Forget your [individual] self and secretly practice. Become one with the true self. The true self is the same as the whole universe. It is a continuation of the Buddha. You don't need enlightenment; to just forget your self and practice secretly, you have to grasp your true self. You must know who you truly are.[8]

---

[6] Ibid., 336.

[7] Ibid., 292–95.

[8] Ibid., vol. 2, 301.

Just get into this position, sit, and see. All the sutras are doctoral theses. They are nothing but theses on zazen for which you only have to sit. That is the "transmission outside the teaching." Zazen is not a part of thought. It is not something written. Zazen is practicing the Buddha Way. It is practicing the Buddha Dharma. It is the "transmission outside the scriptures and beyond words."[9]

"Zazen is like the vast sea, a world without limits; it shines like the moon, spreading its limitless light. " This is [Dōgen] famously extolling zazen.

When I'm asked what is the purpose of zazen, I have to say no purpose. As I've often said, sit, body upright, backbone stretched, breathing through your nose, mouth closed, eyes open, sitting resolutely. . . . Zazen is basically becoming intimate with the self—the Dharma of becoming you. All the sutras are literally extensions of zazen.[10]

It is written in the *Zazen Counsel of Wanshi Zenji:* "It shines without confronting objects." This was written nine hundred years ago. Zazen has since been smeared with lots of bugs. It's said that you do zazen to become enlightened. If you don't get enlightened zazen has no use. So all kinds of ideas and concepts arise and one tries this and that until one penetrates various subjects. Then you have many people believing they've attained enlightenment. Back then, Wanshi Zenji's "It shines without confronting objects," meant it shines on the boundless universe, which is to say that zazen teaches us to just do zazen.

The sun just shines, not for any reason. . . . It just shines. It's "just shining" is the greatness of the sun.

This is the meaning of practice. Practice means "one direction taking in everything." With "one direction taking in everything," it just shines. You just sit. In the Sōtō sect we have the expression shikan taza. There is deep meaning in this "just sitting." In just sitting, satori is there even though you don't say it. Satori is a part of just sitting. This is "one direction taking in everything."

Dōgen Zenji expressed it as "In non-thinking it [Buddha Dharma] manifests." When you are just sitting, there are no thoughts like, "enlightenment will come little by little." That's where Buddha Dharma manifests. As long as you just sit, that is where the Way is. This does

---

[9] Ibid., 303.
[10] Ibid., 310.

not only apply to sitting. When you are helping someone, you just help. You don't say, "If I help her I will gain merit" and you don't take care of someone because it's beneficial. Without thinking such things, you just help whether it brings you benefit or not.[11]

Our bodies do not belong to us. They are the true activity of the life of the great universe. That is to say, our bodies are the great universal life. The proof that this body is the life of the universe is in zazen. In zazen, you place your hands like this and cross your legs and do nothing at all with regard to yourself. By doing zazen in this manner, your body will become the reality of the great universe.[12]

Zazen is an activity that is an extension of the universe. Zazen is not the life of an individual; it is the universe that is breathing.[13]

○

Sawaki led a life in conformity with the philosophy he preached. He was poor throughout his life, he had little interest in material comforts, and he showed no desire for rank or honors. The Chinese Zen Master Rinzai's "Man of no rank" describes Sawaki well.

Sawaki's insistence that zazen comes to nothing seems essential to the Zen world today. "My sermons are criticized by certain audiences," he wrote. "They say that my sermons are hollow, not holy. I agree with them because I myself am not holy. The Buddha's teaching guides people to the place where there is nothing special. . . . People often misunderstand faith as a kind of ecstasy of intoxication. . . . True faith is sobering up from such intoxication."[14] In attempting to take the mystique out of Zen, Sawaki also abjured the awe in which Zen masters were held. Sawaki and his disciples Uchiyama and Yokoyama refused to set themselves up as psychological authorities. They ask us, as did the Buddha, to be lights unto ourselves.

---

[11] Ibid., vol. 2, 328, 329.

[12] *Dōgen Zen Sankyū* (Dōgen Zen Studies) (Tokyo: Chikuma Shobō, 1982), edited by Sakai Tokugen, 282.

[13] Ibid., 208.

[14] Kōdō Sawaki, *The Zen Teaching of "Homeless" Kōdō*, translated by Kōshi Ichida and Shohaku Okumura (Kyoto: Kyoto Sōtō Zen Center, 1990), 72.

3 KŌZAN KATŌ

THE FIRST WAVE OF WESTERNERS

The first group of Westerners started to appear at Antaiji in the late 1960s. America was in the midst of the sixties revolution, an exciting time to be around. Most of us, however, had spent our formative years during the fifties—a transition period characterized by the rise of the Beat Generation. The average age of the group was close to thirty, and the "new age," for most of us, was still very new. We were a mixed bag of misfits—from hippies, beats, and even a former hobo to some rather conventional types—in search of values by which to live. Because of this unusual mixture, few of our expectations, for ourselves or for each other, were set in stone. We were a loose-knit community trying to understand our hosts and each other.

When I first arrived at Gentaku, no one overpowered me with attention, and yet most people extended helping hands in various unobtrusive ways. Uchiyama welcomed me at Antaiji and told me that I could live at the temple or move to a place in the neighborhood and work part time. He seemed to know that I would eventually want to leave the temple grounds and be independent. After my first two months living at Antaiji, I was ready to move into the community of Gentaku. Ellen found me an apartment; Ray gave me his bedding, as he had just moved into Daitokuji Monastery and no longer needed it; Steve and Arlene gave me plates and silverware; and Tom found me my first teaching job.

The apartment Ellen found was in a small two-story building called Hiromisō. She lived on the other end of the complex, and her reasons for having me there were not altogether altruistic.

"Which night do you want for your bath night?" she asked as I went with her to look at the place.

"I don't understand."

"Tsuchihachisō (the other apartment complex that housed foreigners around Antaiji) has no bath so we have to provide at least two nights. Now that there are two of us, we can each provide one night."

"So that's why you were excited about me moving in here?"

Ellen just smiled.

"Thursday night is fine."

Japanese baths in private homes are usually from three to four foot square, and deep enough for you to sit in with the water up to your neck. The area outside of the tub has drainage so you can wash your body before getting into the bath. The bath is for soaking your body once you've washed. That's why many people can use the same tub without changing the water and without the subsequent users finding too much grime in it. We even used the leftover water the next day to do our laundry, as it was usually still warm and we didn't have washing machines. Still, it was quite an adjustment for the few Japanese in our group, who had to get used to the smell of Westerners' body odor, which was quite a bit stronger than that of the Japanese. I remember overhearing a conversation between Kesae and Yuko, wives of two Americans who lived at Tsuchihachisō, while I was relaxing in the bath. Kesae had arrived at Ellen's house on bath night a few minutes after Yuko.

"Who's in the bath?" Kesae asked.

"Smells like Arthur," was Yuko's response.

Japanese sensitivity to smells has always seemed extreme to me. I was told that the rare Japanese with a strong body odor might resort to a very expensive operation to have some of his sweat glands removed. For years I tried to understand why Japanese referred to certain foods that were foreign to them as *kusai*, or "stinking." Turkey and lamb are two examples. I might resist a food because of its unusual taste, but for Japanese it was more commonly a smell that repelled.

To prepare the bath you wash the tub and then fill it with water. Once it is full, you turn on a gas burner and heat up the water. There are wooden boards or a plastic cover that you place on top of the bath to keep the heat in when nobody is in it. You have to be careful to make sure the gas burner was turned off before you drain the water or you could burn the tub and even start a fire. The greatest fear of the Japanese is fire. Most of the houses are constructed of wood and paper, and fire has been a real danger throughout Japanese history. Landlords who rented to foreigners worried that their non-Japanese tenants wouldn't exercise the same caution with fire that Japanese did.

Once during a sesshin two Europeans stayed in my house for the five days while I stayed at Antaiji. The landlady told me that they had left the burners on after the water was drained and only noticed it when they smelled wood burning. They almost burned down the house. I was grateful that she let me back into the apartment after that.

As the number of foreigners increased at Antaiji, we started using the public baths more often. I consider the public baths one of Japan's greatest contributions to civilization. To this day whenever I return to Japan I go to the public baths. My in-laws think I'm a bit crazy to walk ten minutes to a public bath when they have a bath in their home, but watching people greet each other, discuss business, politics, sports, and family matters while washing their hair or soaking in the tub or drying themselves and waiting for their spouses and children to finish gives me the sense of community I felt on bath night at Hiromisō.

In the early days when we had bath nights, people brought cookies and the host provided tea, and we talked and joked and then went home, a lot cleaner—provided you weren't the last to get in the tub.

Another advantage Hiromisō had over Tsuchihashisō was flush toilets. We weren't looking for comfort and some even liked the idea of "roughing it," but there were times when flush toilets came in handy. One day Steve knocked on my door and asked if he could use my toilet. Tsuchihashisō was only a minute away but I thought it might be an emergency and didn't ask questions. When he left, he thanked me and told me that he was looking for his tooth.

"You're looking for your *what*?"

"My false tooth. I swallowed it last night. I have this English student who is a dentist. When this tooth that I broke as a kid fell out last year, he insisted on replacing it for me. He wanted to do a special favor for me. He's put it back a few times but it keeps falling out. He doesn't charge me but he must do it as cheaply as possible. I guess I should go to another dentist and pay so I can complain to him if it falls out again."

Steve's girlfriend Arlene loved telling the story of how she woke up in the middle of the night to the sound of Steve crashing on the floor.

"The feeling of the tooth going down his throat woke him up," she said between laughs. "He was trying to stand on his head to get the tooth back into his mouth, but he kept falling down,"

After three mornings of his regular visit to my toilet rummaging through the previous day's meals with no success, he finally gave up.

Those of us who came to Gentaku to sit at Antaiji realized the need to learn

Japanese as quickly as possible. Uchiyama spoke no English, and speaking through an interpreter left us a step removed from direct contact with the man who was such an important reason for our presence at Antaiji. One monk, Ippei, and two foreigners, Steve and Tom, were available and willing to interpret when needed. They also interpreted special lectures Uchiyama gave for the foreigners. The first talk I attended was translated by all three, though it was Steve, the graduate in Japanese studies at the University of Michigan, who took charge. When the translation didn't seem clear, Ippei and Tom would chime in with their rendition of Uchiyama's statement.

Steve never looked comfortable in the interpreter's role, though I know he enjoyed the challenge. Words didn't flow eloquently from him, but he was clear and to the point. He had an extremely sharp mind and wasn't satisfied with vagueness in his interpretation.

Once a week, a small group of us would get together in Steve's apartment and study Uchiyama's lecture for an hour or two. Steve sat next to the big old reel-to-reel tape recorder with his hand near the switch. He turned it on and Uchiyama's voice declared: "*Wareware wa are ka kore ka to funbetsu suru nōryoku ga aru no da kara.* . . ."

And Steve would switch the machine off.

Arthur: "We distinguish the efficiency. . . "

Steve: "No."

Greg: "We are here and there and . . . "

Steve: "No."

Lew: "We discriminate because . . . "

Steve: "No."

Silence.

Steve: "Because we have the ability to distinguish between this and that . . . "

Click. On goes the tape recorder for the next phrase.

It was as congenial a learning atmosphere as I've ever experienced. Except for Steve and Tom, we knew next to no Japanese, and even they did not pretend to have mastered the language. Steve took charge because he was most proficient. He was serious about helping us understand Uchiyama's words. This serious-looking, wiry little man with penetrating eyes, usually dressed in jeans two sizes too big for him, was a very private person, and it took a few beers to bring him out. When he did get drunk, he had the ability to keep a room full of partygoers entertained with songs and a funny, crude standup comedy routine. The Japanese, generally a reserved people, can get pretty rambunctious when they have a little beer or sake in them. When they do, they are given a great deal of latitude, and nothing is ever mentioned of their outrageous behavior the following day. Even at the temples—or perhaps particularly at the temples—after an extended practice period, monks got plastered and become boisterous, some even licentious; then the following day it would be back to temple life as usual. I believe that this was one aspect of Japanese society that made Steve feel comfortable. He was far more like his hosts than he would ever be willing to admit.

As the members of our small group living in Gentaku met and made friends with other Westerners living in Kyoto, our occasional parties moved to different locations to accommodate our growing numbers. One large space we sometimes used was an old abandoned nunnery rented by a Belgium woman and an American man, Marcel and Sal. The nunnery had a large thatched roof; a traditional earth-floor kitchen, soot-blackened from years of cooking on wood-burning stoves; a few small rooms serving as living quarters; and two large common rooms, one with a finely lacquered Buddhist altar in the middle. The only modern utility was electricity. Water was pumped from a well and the toilets were holes in the ground. The building was surrounded by a garden long untended, which in turn was surrounded by a tall hedge isolating it from the adjoining temple, with which it was associated. The building combined traditional beauty and a funky, run-down atmosphere.

Once during a party at the nunnery some of us were dancing in a room that had a few old tatami (straw floor mats). One started to cave under Steve's feet as, under the influence of beer and sake, he was absorbed in a wild, drunken dance. When he realized that the tatami was about to cave in, he got excited and jumped up and down even harder to insure its collapse.

The next party at the old nunnery was my wedding party. I had started seeing Hiroko during my second year in Japan. We first met at the university where I taught part time. She was studying Pure Land Buddhism, but her passion was for painting. She was studying a form of Japanese painting called Nihonga. A year later we decided to marry.

Western men and Japanese women formed couples quite commonly—much more so than Japanese men and Western women. Many Japanese women, having become more aware of liberated lifestyles in the West, started to feel suffocated by the expectations placed upon them when they married to raise children, clean house and, most importantly, subordinate themselves to their husband's needs. The more independent type of women felt this to be extremely limiting.

Many Western men, at the same time, enjoyed the apparent passiveness and motherly attention they received from Japanese women. The combination of a woman wanting to be liberated and a man attracted to her domestic sensibilities sounds like a formula for disaster. Surprisingly, in most of the situations that I knew of, it wasn't.

We were to get married in Hiroko's father's Pure Land Buddhist temple, with a relatively informal ceremony—though not informal enough for most of my Western friends. Only Mike the artist, who loved to observe all sides of Japanese life, was willing to attend the official ceremony. I decided to hold a separate party for the rest of the crew, and the nunnery was the perfect place. Of course, that meant a play as well. A week before the party, with a few beers in him, Steve announced: "Last time we smashed the floor; this time it will be the whole house."

That made me nervous, as I felt responsible for the place. I heard that Marcel and Sal were planning to move out, and I went to them to confirm that they were leaving.

"Why?" Sal asked.

"Because Steve talked about wrecking the place." I said innocently.

"We don't want the place wrecked whether we leave or not," he responded.

I felt like a fool asking such a question. I assured him I would see to it that nothing went amiss.

It was a wild party, and people from all over Kyoto showed up. I remember someone walking past me, smiling, and saying to me: "Great party man. Who's getting married anyway?"

"I don't know," was all I could think to say.

The accompanying play was about a baby being kidnapped for ransom by some *yakuza* (Japanese Mafia). Later the baby, Rowen, a man from Gentaku in his midthirties dressed in diapers, said it was weeks before his Japanese wife Kesae forgave him for embarrassing her so. The kidnappers had real German Lugers, no longer working of course, supplied by a Japanese lady whose husband must have obtained them during the war. The crowd loved the play and went wild, booing the bad guys and rooting for the baby when he got ornery. They got even wilder when a fuse blew and the lights went out. By the time the lights were finally restored, we were all too drunk to continue the play—beer having played a large part in helping most of us get over our stage fright. But the party continued and people went back to dancing and mingling.

At some point in the evening, Steve came across another weak tatami mat and started getting wild. As he was jumping up and down on it, I asked him to cool it, but he was out of control and I lost patience with him. When he wouldn't stop, I lifted him up and threw him physically out of the room. His light frame was easy to lift and his intoxicated mind offered no resistance. Mike, who has an eye for these memorable moments, has often described how Steve, while flying threw the air, managed to swing his foot through the paper door for one last bit of destruction as he sailed out of the room with a big smile across his face.

The second year I was at Antaiji, Tom and Yuko went to spend a year in the States. Ippei left Antaiji to study Japanese sword fighting (Kendō) with the Zen and martial arts teacher Ōmori Sōgen. As a result Steve was the only one left to interpret for the foreign community when someone wished to speak to Uchiyama. He also spent a lot of time editing Uchiyama's first book for foreigners, *An Approach to Zen*, which he and Tom had translated. This was to be Steve's last major contribution in the service of Uchiyama and Antaiji in Japan, but it was eventually followed by an even more important service for the temple and Uchiyama, though not in Japan.

After my marriage, my wife Hiroko, Steve, and I decided to move to a farmhouse in the country about thirty miles outside of Kyoto. Mizuhochō was the name of a village near a small temple run by Dōyū, a disciple of Uchiyama's. Dōyū introduced us to a member of his parish, Kiku, a municipal worker and the eldest son of the owner of a futon shop, who rented an old country farmhouse in a valley outside of Mizuhochō. Dōyū told him that we were looking to live in the country and Kiku invited us to share his house with him. He said he didn't stay there often, and that we could live there for three thousand yen a month. Split two ways this was quite reasonable and it allowed me to keep my rental in Kyoto; I worked in Kyoto on Wednesday and needed a place to stay there. Steve, however, gave up his Kyoto apartment. I've never known him to hold on to anything he wasn't presently using. He owned one pair of pants, which, he once told me, he wore until it was time for a new pair. That time, he said, was when the old pair needed to be washed.

Steve owned a small van. We packed our belongings and two very reluctant cats into his van and headed for the country. The house, an old thatched-roof farmhouse, was in a narrow valley that got very little sun. The kitchen had an earth floor and wood-burning stoves. There was no chimney, and the smoke from the stoves floated up to the thatched roof and seeped into the straw, which was supposed to make the thatch last longer.

Our daily lives at the farmhouse were not what Kiku had envisioned. Steve and I got up at 5:00 AM to do zazen. We followed the Antaiji schedule of fifty-minute sittings and ten minutes of walking meditation. We finished sitting by ten. Hiroko, who wasn't interested in sitting, prepared breakfast. At about 10:30, while we were eating on the porch, an old man would come by.

"Is it lunchtime already?" He would ask, looking a bit surprised.

"No. It's half past ten," one of us would reply.

"Oh," he would say and return to his work.

His work was to trim the trees and collect the scrub from the mountain in back of our house. He didn't have to work, but he seemed to enjoy it. He told us that he was eighty-four years old and that he was born in the farmhouse. He was now living with his son and daughter-in-law in their new home in the center of Mizuhochō. He had been a rice farmer and very likely a *burakumin*, or member of the traditional outcaste class. Dōyū once mentioned that *burakumin* lived in this area.

There was a large Buddhist altar in the far wall of the largest room in the house that indicated by its design that the family were followers of the Jōdo Shin, or True Pure Land, sect of Japanese Buddhism, which teaches the superiority of faith in "other power" (*tariki*) over one's own efforts. Many members of the outcaste class, powerless to help themselves in society, embraced this sect of Buddhism. The fact that the farmer's land was located in a narrow valley that received little sun was another hint to the fact that they may have been *burakumin*. When land was parceled out centuries earlier, the outcastes were given the poorest land with the least sun.

Times had changed, though, and the old man's son established a successful electrical contracting company and made enough money to build a new house in a better part of town. But the old man wasn't impressed with the new house and didn't seem ready to settle down in front of the television for the rest of his life. He also knew that everyone got up early, had breakfast, went to work and ate lunch at noon. So when he saw us eating long after what he knew was the proper breakfast time, he could only assume that we were having lunch. And lunchtime meant that it must be noon.

Day after day, we would eat at ten thirty, and every day he would ask us if it was noon already. Answering this question daily and watching this old man clear brush and trim trees on the mountain in back of the house became a treasured part of our daily routine. He was one of a dying breed—rugged, hardworking, and a lover of the land. His family, too, embraced this work ethic. While his son ran the electrical contracting company, his daughter-in-law, along with raising the children and feeding the family, worked in the remaining rice paddies that the family owned. Small but rugged, she was out there at planting time with her work clothes, high boots, and hat and scarf to protect her from the sun, planting seedlings by hand, one by one.

After our daily brunches, Steve worked on a piece of land he was preparing for a vegetable garden, and Hiroko took out her sketchpad and started drawing. Kiku dropped by once in a while, but he always seemed bothered by something.

Sometimes we took walks in the wood near the house, where we picked windfalls from the chestnut trees. We took turns cooking dinner, after which we chopped wood, prepared the bath, read, and went to bed. It was winter, and like all the other families in the village, we collected persimmons and hung them to dry.

Once when we returned back from our monthly sesshin in Kyoto, Kiku was there with his girlfriend. Kiku had introduced us to Yumi when we first moved into the house. She was single and lived with her son. A tall, graceful woman, her hair hung down to her waist. Her demeanor made her seem out of place in this small farming village. Kiku told us proudly that she was a potter. She seemed friendly when we first met her, but when we surprised Kiku and Yumi that day with our sudden appearance, she left without saying a word to us. The next time Kiku came by it was to ask us to leave.

I asked Kiku what the problem was and he went into a hysterical tirade. All I can remember of it now was his one legitimate complaint: We had fed the cats from one of his beautiful pottery dishes. We didn't leave. The next time we returned from a work trip to Kyoto, we found all our belongings dumped outside on the ground.

I was fuming, and even Steve kept asking me to teach him how to throw a punch. Hiroko directed her energy toward calming me down, and in the end we left peacefully because we didn't want to cause trouble for Dōyu or the owners.

When we said our goodbyes to the old man and his family as we left town, we mentioned to the son the incident with Kiku. That's when we learned that Kiku hadn't paid him any rent. The son didn't hide his disgust for Kiku, and when we returned to visit some months later, we learned that Kiku was evicted a week after we left. We also learned that the old man had died and the son sold the house. We were sad to have left before our persimmons dried but glad not to have been around when the old man died and the house was sold.

Though Steve spent the next six months in Kyoto going from house to house, renting temporary places and living with friends, he never found a permanent place to live. His last real home in Japan was our thatched roof farmhouse in the country.

Steve's last service to Uchiyama and Antaiji was in America. He was now in Kyoto with no place to live. When Uchiyama asked one of his disciples, Kōshi Ichida, to move to America to help a group of Americans who had previously sat with another Antaiji monk in North Hampton, Massachusetts, Steve agreed to assist him. Having no home at the time, and feeling a bit tired of Japanese life, Steve decided that it might be a good time to move on. Just as he played a pivotal role in helping the foreign community communicate with Uchiyama at Antaiji, he was crucial in helping Ichida set up the Pioneer Valley Zendō in Charlemont Massachusetts. Kōshi had studied English in Japan in preparation for this new assignment and had met many Americans in his four years at Antaiji. Neither his English ability nor his contact with Americans in Japan was sufficient, however, to allow him to deal with the intricacies of the bureaucracy involved in starting a not-for-profit temple in America. Steve's ability in Japanese and English, and his relish for new and challenging projects, prepared him for this role.

Kōshi had studied Japanese sword fighting for many years, had four years of Zen training at a Rinzai Zen temple before coming to Antaiji, and had studied shipbuilding at a merchant marine college. He was talented with his hands and devoted to his teacher's way. Like Steve, he appeared to be the perfect choice to transmit the practice Uchiyama had developed at Antaiji to Americans in the United States. Kōshi and Steve were given money to buy land in order to set up a practice place of their own. They bought five acres of land in a fairly remote part of the country, about fifty miles northwest of North Hampton. They started clearing land and building on it while living in a tent.

While Steve and Kōshi were busy building the temple everything seemed to be going well, but when it came time to run the temple difficulties arose. The hierarchy of Zen, the conservative nature of people from Kyoto, and the strong wills of two very talented men from very different cultures caused a parting of the ways, and Steve ended up completely severing ties with Antaiji.

This was not his plan when his relationship with Kōshi became difficult. However, on returning to Japan, he went to talk with Uchiyama about an unclear passage in a book of Uchiyama's that Steve was translating. Rather than look into the passage together, Uchiyama told him that he was right and suggested he write his own interpretation of the text rather than translate Uchiyama's. To Steve, who had almost completed the translation, to be told to drop the project and write his own book was quite a disappointment. I don't know what Uchiyama was thinking at the time, but he certainly wasn't considering the amount of work Steve put into the book. Uchiyama had the power in this situation, and there was little Steve could do about it. Considering the service he gave to Antaiji and Uchiyama over the years, this final act of Uchiyama's seems to have been enough to make Steve wash his hands of the whole Antaiji scene.

One day, early on in my stay in Japan, I dropped in on Steve in his Tsuchihashisō apartment. He was sitting with a manuscript in hand that he had received from Uchiyama. We greeted each other with our typical non-greeting greeting—mutual eye contact and maybe a grunt of a "hi," and I sat down on a cushion he flipped over to me.

"Can you imagine? This guy calls Sawaki a scholar." he said.

I didn't know much about Sawaki at the time, but I quickly gathered that he was anything but a scholar—somewhat of a dirty word at Antaiji. I also realized that this "guy" Steve referred to, whoever he was, must be a pretty interesting character if he could refer to Sawaki disparagingly as a scholar.

Steve continued, "This guy Katō is a friend of Sawaki, man, and he wants to split from this temple together with Sawaki because the temple is bad news. But he complains that Sawaki can't leave because he has too many books and they will weigh him down on the road."

"Where'd you get that book?"

"Uchiyama gave it to me."

Uchiyama must have been given the manuscript to comment on, as he was a leading figure in the Sawaki Zen lineage. Sawaki played an important role in helping Katō survive during the World War II years in Japan.

I finally picked up the book in an old Buddhist bookstore in Kyoto a couple of years later. It was titled *Zazen ni Ikiru* (Living in Zazen) and was a book about the life of another colorful Zen character, who literally lived for zazen.

Every time I read about a dynamic Zen teacher I found myself returning to thoughts about Uchiyama, my teacher. My question as to whether he was an authentic Zen master had never really been resolved. I had come to place more and more emphasis on the practice of zazen and concerned myself less about the naïve question of whether he was really "enlightened." But the question never completely disappeared.

A group of us once engaged in a long discussion about whether Uchiyama's or Yokoyama's style of Zen was more authentic. Everyone had a loudly voiced opinion about which was the more legitimate. Finally, Steve, getting a bit tired of the foolishness, shouted, "Uchiyama is Uchiyama and Yokoyama is Yokoyama." That was the end of the discussion.

It had been almost three years since I last saw Tesshō. My head was full of Kōzan Katō, having just read the account of his life that Steve had talked about, and I was curious whether Tesshō knew of him and what he thought of the old Zen master. When I called his brother's temple, I was given his new address. He was living in a small two-room flat on the second floor of an apartment house in Kumagaya, a city in Saitama Prefecture just north of Tokyo. I went to Kumagaya, promptly got lost, and finally found his apartment with the help of a few friendly citizens. It was in a newly developed section of town with no particular character. When I arrived at the apartment building, I looked up and saw on the second floor balcony a bald-headed guy in *samue*, monk's work clothes, hanging out his wash on a clothesline.

"Tesshō," I called out from the street.

"Arthur, come on up. I'll be through in a minute," he said, continuing to hang his socks and underwear on the line.

I waited by the door for him to finish hanging out his clothes and then followed him into his apartment. It was small, the only furniture a low table and bookshelves in the living room and a *zafu* and *zaniku*—a sitting cushion and square mat—in the bedroom. The bookshelves were full and piles of books were stacked around it. I wondered if his experience with Ban Roshi and his time at Eiheiji had embittered him toward temple life.

I knew that Ban wanted me as a disciple because I was a foreigner. As absurd as it felt to me for a Zen master to be seeking name and fame, it was hard to rationalize Ban's actions as anything other than that. In the middle of the Morioka sesshin the zendō was invaded by a local television crew. As I went into my interview with the Roshi, the strobe lights were shining on me and one of the crew actually moved me to a different spot so that he could get a better shot. Ban apparently had no objection to all of this. That night, accompanied by the Roshi, we all went into a room in the temple where a television was playing the evening news. There I saw myself on the screen entering the dokusan room bowing to Roshi.

"Your new temple looks more austere than Tōshōji," I said jokingly.

"True. Ban Roshi probably couldn't live here, could he?" And we both laughed.

Tesshō told me that Ban corralled him into becoming a disciple.

"After my father died, a friend of his, an executive of the national railroad became my mentor and a kind of guardian. He knew of my interest in philosophical matters and so introduced me to Ban Roshi. When I had a breakthrough during my first sesshin, Ban Roshi asked me to take ordination. It was my first real experience with Zen and I didn't feel I could refuse Roshi's request."

I wasn't sure whether Tesshō was implying that he accepted Ban's offer because of a sense of obligation to his sponsor, who had introduced him to the Roshi, or because of his kenshō. But at any rate Tesshō felt he had been pressured into shaving his head, and the experience made him cautious about making another Zen commitment.

He took a couple of beers out of the refrigerator and poured us each a glass.

"How did you end up here? I asked.

"I was practicing alone on a nearby mountain and a friend of mine visited me there. He told me of a doctor's son who needed a fulltime tutor. The boy had become unmanageable and the mother and father were in a quandary as to what to do. They hoped that a monk might be able to straighten him out.

"I agreed to take the job and the family got me this apartment walking distance from the clinic that the father owned and ran."

With a lull in the conversation, I jumped in with the question that had been occupying me during the trip to Kumagaya.

"Have you ever heard of Kōzan Katō?" I asked.

"Yes, of course. He was quite a Zen man."

I wasn't surprised that he had, and was happy that he thought very highly of him.

"You know, I had a chance to study with him and I blew it," he said.

"How was that?" I asked.

"Ban Roshi, of all people, asked me to meet with him in 1969, when Katō was about ninety-three years old. I'd never heard of him then, and I thought to myself, 'What's the use of meeting a ninety-three-year-old monk? He must be feeble.' I could kick myself for blowing such an opportunity."

He poured me another glass of beer, and, as is the custom, I took the bottle and filled his in return.

"Did your experiences at Tōshōji and Eiheiji sour you to temple life?" I asked.

"Not really. I trained at a temple in Kyūshū for almost two years after that. The Roshi took a special liking to me and was even hoping I would take over when he was ready to retire."

"Why did you leave?"

"I saw what he had to do as head of the temple, and I knew I wanted no part of that. It's not easy being a Roshi. You don't just train monks, you know. It's a political position. You have to get involved in all kinds of activities in the community. There are a lot of petty fights among parishioners, too, that you have to deal with. That's not for me."

I kept noticing parallels in Tesshō's attitude to that of Kōzan Katō's. Both had started off in Sōtō temples but, dissatisfied with the lack of seriousness, switched to Rinzai Zen. Both ran away from the opportunity to become heads of training monasteries. In both cases, it wasn't clear to me whether they were simply purists or afraid of responsibility or both.

"But I learned a lot from the training there," he continued. I decided to try to practice without lying down. I managed to continue that way for a year."

"One year?" I said, trying to sound casual. I'd heard of monks of old who practiced in that way, but it always seemed to me to be a crazy, macho approach to Zen.

"You know up until then I was always critical of monks who dozed during zazen. I guess I was a bit smug about it because I never dozed. Well, after practicing for a while without lying down, I started dozing quite a bit. I finally realized what dozing during zazen was all about.

"I also got pretty deeply into koan training. It wasn't like at Ban's place. I spent every minute of the day working on my koan. When I was cutting vegetables, I would work on it. It was driving my crazy. I would start repeating it and would get so frustrated that the recitation would turn into a cursing tirade against my teacher. I would find myself mumbling, 'That dirty bastard,' under my breath. But whenever I had a breakthrough, the Roshi would know as soon as I entered the dokusan room. I wouldn't have to say anything.

"When I left the temple, Roshi told me I could come back anytime I wanted. He really gave me special treatment. I knew I had to leave, but I still felt pretty depressed when I finally did go. I remember wandering the country after that, begging and finding cheap lodging wherever I could, and feeling lousy.

"Once, as I was traveling in Hiroshima, I sat by a railroad station eating my lunch and feeling pretty down. I started watching a group of small kids playing ball. Some of them came over to me and asked, 'Ikkyū-san, you want to join us?'[1]

"I started playing with them for a while. I had a train ticket and was planning to travel east, making my way back to Odawara. Ten minutes before my train was scheduled to leave, I said goodbye to the kids and went into the station. As I was about to board the train I could see the kids outside in a huddle discussing something. They were digging into their pockets and counting their money. Those who didn't have enough were borrowing from those who had a little extra. Finally, they went to the ticket counter and bought thirty-yen tickets, which allowed them to go on to the platform. As I was leaving, they all ran onto the platform and started waving their hands and calling, 'Goodbye, Ikkyū-san!' They picked me up right out of my depression."

I spent the night at Tesshō's apartment and left the next morning for Kyoto. I was inspired with new energy to practice. Uchiyama and Antaiji grew in stature as I thought about people like Tetsugyū Ban and Tōshōji. Had it not been for Uchiyama, I never would have known of Kōzan Katō.

O

KŌZAN KATŌ ROSHI

How can I describe a priest as enigmatic as Kōzan Katō? He is the only Zen teacher in this story who went through Rinzai Zen training—at the strictest Zen monastery of the time, to boot—and came out with nothing but praise for the brutal treatment he received. In fact, he praised just about everything, though nothing more highly or with greater vigor than zazen.

Moreover, Katō's teaching is not severe at all. He gets people to do zazen because his love for the practice is infectious. In every photo of him except those capturing him doing zazen or practicing calligraphy, his toothless mouth is open wide in laughter. He is the reincarnation of Hotei, the laughing Buddha.

I am listening to tapes that Katō's son Taigan sent me of his father lecturing at a zazen meeting at the temple of a disciple in northern Japan. The trip was a long one and

---

[1] Ikkyū Sōjun (1394–1481) was an eccentric Zen monk who became a legend. Stories of his cleverness as a child became the inspiration for comics and an animated television show, and most children in Japan were familiar with him, so that the sight of a Zen monk immediately brought Ikkyū to mind.

Katō was ninety years old at the time. Though I call these "lectures," they certainly don't resemble any traditional Zen Buddhist lecture.

Katō begins: "Well, now, it's like . . . since I've reached my ninetieth year, I'm getting more and more feeble. . . . " After some more stammering, he continues, "My old lady said to me, 'Give it up,' trying to stop me from coming. She said, 'It's really dangerous. You can hardly hear and you've become quite feeble. You'd better not go. You'll only end up being a burden on everyone.'"

Then he talked about the joy of being ninety, knowing this might be his last year of life, and he suggested that everyone practice zazen as a farewell to him.

Katō is truly uncomfortable lecturing, so he just rambles. But when students ask him questions about zazen or Buddhism at the end of the meeting, the rambling stops. He becomes sharp and clear.

"Do zazen. It is not difficult. Zazen is the most important thing in a person's life. Do it everyday and you will see. Zazen is not something done only when you cross your legs. You have to do zazen that is not separated from your daily life. Whatever you do, don't lose the composure that you felt when you did zazen. Your daily life should be based on the order that comes from zazen—the feeling of regulating the body and mind. It must work in your life. Do it for five minutes or three minutes, but do it everyday. Make it a habit."

His voice is soft and joyful. If Sawaki is yang, Katō is yin. There is a Buddhist expression "rōba Zen," or "grandmotherly Zen." There is no better expression of the Zen of this twentieth-century Hotei.

○

LIVING IN ZAZEN

The story, as I heard it from a Buddhist scholar named Kiyoshi Hoshi, was that Ryūmin Akizuki, Zen priest and scholar, went to Zeze-an, Katō's temple in Okutama, Tokyo, with a small hidden tape recorder. He listened to Katō, who was ninety-four years old at the time, tell the story of his life, and then he brought home the recording and transcribed it. This record was subsequently published as *Living in Zazen*. The story of the hidden tape recorder may have been fabricated to add to Katō's mystique, but his story is compelling enough without this preface, for it is also the history of Japanese Zen in the early twentieth century.

> I was born in the Kurozasa Mountains in Mikawa. I left my hometown when my father went to Nagoya to start a sake-making business. I was named Sanjirō and was the fourth of ten children.

> My father's sake business failed. When I was nine years old, a new bridge was completed in some distant place and I was taken to the festivities in celebration of the event. I was then dropped off at a temple and left there. The temple was a mile or so from my house, so I couldn't return home. I thought something was peculiar when my father had my head shaved before we left home for the festivities. I'd become a novice monk at the Zen temple Daieiji north of Nagoya, but not as a result of any personal aspiration. My father had deceived me, making me a prisoner of the temple.

Katō opens the account of his life by de-romanticizing his relationship to Buddhism; the anecdote also shows that his faith grew out of his practice and not from any initial belief.

His early life at the temple, especially his studies, was painful.

> After having been given over to the temple, I was hardly ever permitted to go to school. Instead, I had to learn Chinese classics by rote. This was a long time ago.[2] Three of us—an old lady and two novice monks—used to gather around a paper lantern. The old lady spun cotton and the two of us sat along side her and studied. We read sutras and the Chinese classics. The Chinese characters in them were difficult for young elementary-school students, but we managed to learn them. If we didn't memorize them, we got bopped on the head. . . . Putting all our energy into memorization, we lagged behind in our ability to reason. We understood none of the meaning of the text; we simply memorized how to read the characters. We learned according to the proverb, "read mechanically one hundred times and the meaning will come through." After we had made some progress, we had to read the Lotus Sutra. The Chinese characters in this sutra are extremely difficult. It took many years and was a painful experience but we finally memorized it. The process bordered on brutality.

Despite Katō's claim that his ability to reason lagged, he continues by describing how argumentative he became. He even told the head priest of the temple to study modern science to familiarize himself with contemporary thought. They would argue, he said, until the priest ended it with the his usual, "Get the hell out of here."

---

[2] Katō was born in 1875 so this was probably between 1885 and 1890.

Katō dressed in Western clothing even when he went to parishioners' homes to read sutras. He was proud of his liberal ideas and believed he was in complete accord with the progressive trends in religion of that period, but upon reflection he said, "When I think back on those days, [I feel so embarrassed] I break out in a cold sweat."

Though Katō criticized the temple and his teacher, he did learn from the head priest and became emotionally dependent on him. When the head priest died, Katō fell apart. "My mind was scattered," he said, "and I became physically unhealthy; I couldn't sleep at night."

Then he was advised by another monk to practice zazen. Katō was in his early twenties, living in Tokyo at the time, and on this monk's advice he went to Engakuji Temple.

> Sōen Shaku Roshi had returned to Engakuji from America to high acclaim. I went to Engakuji to practice Zen meditation under him. I went there as a layman, not a monk. Sōen had a new style, giving *sanzen* (interviews) sitting on a chair by a table.
>
> I had kenshō after being with Sōen only one week. This upset my Zen practice. I tried two or three check points (*sassho*) and was able to solve them through thinking.[3] Then I started to have doubts. As long as I continued meeting with the teacher, I would pass koans one by one. It was that easy. According to the practice at Engakuji, it was best to do zazen for a short period of time and advance through all the koans within three years. Then you were to study, study, study. If you weren't a good scholar, you received very little attention. I wasn't satisfied with that. Having had a satori so quickly, I had no interest in it. I'd originally been a Sōtō monk and had read Buddhist texts. I had practiced a little too. So with some hint, I quickly understood, and the feeling, "Aha! This is it!" would immediately surface. In the end it was through thinking that I progressed with koans. It didn't deserve to be called Zen. Even studying Buddhist texts and doctrine was better than this kind of halfhearted practice. This was intellectual Zen. I wanted to practice more deeply so I left.

For the next few years Katō described himself as being lost. He returned to his hometown and through his family's wealth and influence (you could buy temples

---

[3] Sassho are questions a teacher asks a student after an initial breakthrough with a koan in order to check that the student really did solve the koan.

then, according to Katō) he inherited a temple. Seeing no relationship between life as a temple priest and true Buddhism, he eventually abandoned his temple. He had come across Dōgen's *Zuimonki* in a bookstore in Nagoya, and he made up his mind to follow the path of zazen. Enduring the wrath of his parents for abandoning the temple they had acquired for him, he set out in search of a place to practice zazen. The security of his own parish, which his parents felt was his passport to a place in society, he saw as an obstacle to a life devoted to zazen.

"At that time there were no Sōtō zendōs where zazen was really being practiced, so I had to go to a Rinzai monastery," Katō recalled. He chose Shōgenji in Ibuka, Minokamo City, Gifu Prefecture, because it was known for the severity of its practice. Having no experience with Rinzai monasteries or the etiquette required there, he spent one night on the way to Ibuka at a small Rinzai temple. He learned all he could from the monk in charge, and set out the next day for Shōgenji. He arrived while a ceremony was being held for its founder. Katō helped out at the ceremony and when it was over, he had to go through the formal *"niwa zume"* (confinement in the garden).

> Though it was only a formality, I had to remain in a prostrate position and wasn't allowed to raise my head. I put my surplice (*kesa*) on the ground and placed my head on it. Since the only thing required of me was that I keep this position, I could have slept. Still, to remain prostrate in the garden all day is quite painful. Once in a while I would go to relieve myself. I'd take off my robe and lay it down neatly and would go to the toilet—that was allowed, so I could take my time and relax. By evening someone would come and say, "Get out!" They usually refuse your request to stay. The monk would say, "No use practicing here, there are better places to practice. Go to one of them!" He'd then beat me while I was prostrate and drive me out with the keisaku.[4] I'd leave and then come right back. Since this was all a formality, he was waiting for me to return. Even now, I believe, niwa zume still exists in most monasteries.
>
> When this was over, I was thrown in a room and kept in a kind of solitary confinement. This practice is called *tanga zume*. There they watched my every move. It was designed for that. They put me in that room and peeped in to observe my behavior, to see if I remained calm and composed. Had I panicked or acted strangely rather than seriously

---

[4] As noted earlier, this is the Rinzai pronunciation of the stick called the kyōsaku in Sōtō Zen.

Sodō Yokoyama sitting in zazen.

Sodō Yokoyama serving tea and playing the grass flute in Kaikoen Park. (Photographs courtesy of Daihōrin Publishers)

Kōdō Sawaki.

Kōdō Sawaki sitting in zazen. (Photograph courtesy of Daihōrin Publishers)

Sawaki with his disciple Kōshō Uchiyama at the old Antaiji garden. (Photograph courtesy of Daihōrin Publishers)

New Year celebration at Tokuunin. Left to right: Kōdō Sawaki, Kōzan Katō, and Sōgen Nakajima.

Kōzan Katō.

Kōzan Katō sitting in zazen at age ninety-three.

Motoko Ikebe at age sixty-six.

Motoko Ikebe, age eighty-three.

Jōshin Kasai.

On the old Antaiji veranda. From left to right: Jōshin Kasai, Shōjō Karako, and head monk Kōhō Watanabe.

In front of the old Antaiji garden. From left to right: Kōhō Watanabe, Shūsoku Kushiya, and Dōyū Takamine.

Sesshin held in Morioka with Tetsugyū Ban. Tesshō is carrying the *kyōsaku*. The author is the second from the left.

The Buddha Hall at the Hamasaka Antaiji.

Kōshō Uchiyama one month before his death.

Kōshō Uchiyama at age sixty-seven in front of his retirement home.

engaging in zazen, they'd have dragged me out of there. This went on for about three days. It was rather easy because I didn't have to do any work. As long as I did zazen, everything was fine. After this I was allowed to sit in the zendō as one of the monks.

Katō goes on to explain the philosophy behind some of these severe Zen monastic practices.

> Once you were accepted in the zendō, you were no longer subject to being beaten and thrown out. They would only revert to that if you did something wrong, disobeyed, or talked back to them. You were required to listen even if what they said was unreasonable. A feudal attitude prevailed there. If you were told by a senior to do something, or to do something in a particular way, you were expected to say yes and go along with it. That's practice. It's getting rid of the ego. If you say this or that, you are responding from a self-centered point of view. The primary objective is to rid you of self-centeredness. There actually is meaning in it after all. At any rate you were never allowed to express your own opinion. You were required to follow this kind of discipline for the first one or two years.

Brian Victoria's book *Zen at War* made me aware of the degree to which this feudal attitude that Katō appears to have supported may have been a product of a military spirit that many Zen Buddhist priests and Zen organizations adhered to. One result of this attitude in the Zen world was to aid the Japanese government by giving them a philosophical foundation to support their suppression of dissent as they marched their country to war in the 1930s.

The impression I got of Katō as a result of reading his dharma talks and records of conversations with friends and disciples, however, was of a man with great ability for self-reflection. While his resolve to practice the Way was firm, he was able to laugh at his own foolishness and at his early mistaken views of Buddhism. But right to the end he believed in a Zen method in which the novice must be completely subordinate to his superior. He considered his superiors good people who had his best intentions at heart.

In his case, that may have been so, but in the political arena, when the term "holy war" was being used to muster support for Japanese military aggression abroad, Katō seems to have been unwilling to cast aside his personal opinions and lend his support to the government—at least when advising his disciples. When counseling his student, Kōen Kureyama, who was on his way to serve in the military during

World War II, he said, "When you kill someone, you can't say it is for a holy war. Never take part in this senseless killing."

Katō talked about the counterproductive effect his knack for solving koans had on his practice: "Shaku Sōen Roshi's recognition of my kenshō was extremely bad for me. Because of that, I didn't follow through to the end. You really must follow through to the end." Though he went to Shōgenji with the intention of doing just that, and though he felt great respect for Dōshū, Shōgenji's Roshi, he once more found koans easy to solve intellectually and again became discouraged and quit. He decided to just sit, without attending dokusans, and he did so for five years. Later, however, he described the decision to just sit until he experienced a true realization as "another self-centered point of view."

Though upon reflection later he saw his behavior at this time as childish and self-centered, to the monks at Shōgenji he appeared to be growing in stature. Ironically, his attachment to his own idea of the meaning of Buddhist practice, which caused him to withdraw from the regular monastery routine, led those around him to regard him as a superior monk.

> Within only five years, I had to deal with the problem of being called upon to be one of the top monastery functionaries. Everyone around me insisted that I take the position, so I had no choice but to leave. I'd asked myself what it would mean to be in charge; would that make me a genuine monk? My ideas were quite inflexible [as to what real Zen practice was] when I left Ibuka [Shōgenji]. I decided to go into the mountains alone and do zazen until I penetrated to its core. As I look at it now, I see it too as another fixed idea.

After leaving Shōgenji, Katō spent the next two years at a nearby mountain, Hazama. There was a valley, a waterfall, and a shrine for ascetics. Though he doesn't say why, after two years on Mount Hazama he left his mountain retreat and went to Eiheiji for the annual lectures on the writings of Dōgen. There he became friends with a senior monk named Kanryō. Ryoei Mizuno, the roshi in charge of Yōsenji, a temple in Matsuzaka City, Mie Prefecture, was a visiting lecturer at the meeting. Mizuno, a scholar-monk who had spent years in America, asked Kanryō and Katō to take charge of his training center. Mizuno felt that since the two of them had trained in Rinzai monasteries, they would train his monks in a strict Rinzai style. Katō wasn't anxious to go but submitted to his respected friend's wishes. Kanryō had completed the Rinzai koan practice and, Katō, though ambivalent about koans, was strongly influenced by him.

Katō describes Kanryō as "very talented, sharp as a razor, and an able poet." His respect for his friend's bearing and ability made him take Kanryō's advice seriously. The men had similar backgrounds, having switched from Sōtō to Rinzai Zen, but Katō seemed on the verge of giving up Rinzai practice, too. The two friends often debated the value of koans, with Kanryō recommending Katō follow through to the end. Katō retorted that there was no meaning in a practice that you can grasp through the intellectual process. Kanryō accused him of holding on to his own opinions. He said Katō couldn't judge koans because he hadn't followed through on them. Then he said something that caught Katō's attention. He said, "Even if it is worthless, complete the practice as though you were throwing things on a garbage heap, but *do* complete it."

Kanryō talked about an extraordinary Zen master named Sanshōken, at Bairinji in Kyūshū. He recommended that Katō study with him. Having been so impressed by his friend's statement about throwing things on a garbage heap, Katō made a complete turnaround: "All right," I said, "then I'll follow through to the end as though I were throwing things on a garbage heap."

It was at this time that Katō became friends with Kōdō Sawaki, who was assistant head of training at Yōsenji. The two monks spent long hours together talking about Zen and developing a friendship that was to last a half a century. Katō and Sawaki talked about leaving Yōsenji, both agreeing that it was not a place for serious practitioners. But Sawaki was astonished at how little time his friend wasted after making his decision to leave. "I was taken by surprise," he was to remark later, "and heard no more of him. Seventeen years later I saw him walking in downtown Kurume with a torn umbrella. I learned then of his journey to Bairinji."

KATŌ GOES TO BAIRINJI

If Katō was looking for a place where his intellectual grasp of koans wouldn't help him, he found it in Bairinji.

Katō was forty when he arrived at Bairinji. At training monasteries seniority was based not on chronological age but on when you arrived at the monastery. He had to swallow his pride and tolerate reprimands from monks as young as seventeen years old who had arrived before him. Monks of petty natures frequently used this rule to lord it over others. One such monk, who had come to Bairinji a year before Katō, always referred to him as "old monk" and ordered him around and scolded him mercilessly. Katō managed to control himself, but just barely. He had come to Bairinji to study under Sanshōken, of whom his friend Kanryō spoke so highly, and he didn't want to spoil his chance to do so. Bairinji was proud of its reputation as a "devil" monastery with harsh discipline, and Katō had to exert great effort to control his feelings.

> I'd come to Bairinji to study under Sanshōken. Though I still held to my own cocky opinion about the meaninglessness of koans, I'd come to Bairinji because Kanryō said I should meet the Roshi. But Sanshōken had already retired and the new teacher was Kōmushitsu. Sanshōken lived in an elegant retreat on the other side of the garden near the river. Only during *rōhatsu* sesshin [a practice period held near December 8, traditionally regarded as the day of the Buddha's enlightenment] did he have koan interviews with the practicing monks. At other times newcomers were not able to approach him. Having come with the intention of meeting him, I found this difficult to bear. The new teacher appeared somewhat unimpressive.

The following story of Katō's first rōhatsu sesshin at Bairinji describes some rather brutal behavior. It's important to keep in mind that Katō, who is the recipient of this vicious treatment, considered the lesson one of the most valuable in his career as a Zen practitioner.

> When the first rōhatsu sesshin came, I told myself not to pass up the opportunity and rushed out [to dokusan], taking the lead. It was interesting how everyone tried to be first, as though it was a race. At Shōgenji, the monks were reluctant to go to dokusan; they clung to their cushions, and the monk in charge had to drag them from their cushions and make them go. But at Bairinji the monks rushed ahead noisily in what one can only call an ill-mannered fashion. As their slippers flew, they rushed out to form a queue to go to the dokusan room. It was a strange practice. I dashed forward like the others and took a front seat in line because, as I said before, I felt I had to see Sanshōken. If I was late, I feared, I might not get the chance.
>
> While we waited in line, an assistant surveyed all of us. He resembled a demon as he came over to me, grabbed me by the neck, and looked at my face. He then said, "Dokusan with Sanshōken is too good for you." Holding me by the neck in front of everyone, he said, "He's too good for you, the new teacher will be just fine." Then he dragged me out.
>
> I thought to myself, "You shithead, I'm not a beginner," but it didn't matter how I felt.

"Get out of here, he's too good for you," he repeated and started beating me with the keisaku. I had to give up and leave. "Well," I thought, "I'll just have to wait until next year." I was really incensed. I did eventually start having dokusan with Sanshōken, but it didn't last very long.

At rōhatsu sesshin the assistants get very worked up and they train the new monks very severely. I thought I appeared humble, but, because of my age—I was already forty years old—they assumed I traveled the monastery circuit for the fun of it. It was not unusual to come across guys like that at Zen monasteries. Though I wasn't that type, they thought I was. So they decided that if they didn't train me severely, I would become difficult to deal with in the end. Consequently, I was trained in my first sesshin with excessive harshness.

Had I merely been beaten, I could have put up with it. At rōhatsu everyone, including lay students, sat in rows. The assistant attacked me with abusive language from the start: "It's useless at age forty to put on airs as though you were enlightened!" That really hurt. "Damn it, you young squirt," I thought. Then he said: "I'll give you a taste of thirty blows from a disciple of Sanshōken!" I thought to myself, "What the hell are you talking about?" but I could do nothing. Then he started hitting me. He actually hit me thirty times. It was a wonder I didn't faint. The keisaku broke in half and went flying. I kept the broken parts for a long time to remember the incident, but now I don't know what I did with them.

Everyone was not treated this way. I was hit thirty or forty times. It was just right for me. I felt as if a heavy burden had been lifted from me. I still feel grateful for that today. I guess, up to that point, being already forty, I had reasoned things out and thought that I had a little insight into Buddhism. I grasped it [Buddhism] in my own way, but I feel my understanding at the time was really little more than my own self-centered thinking after all. Because I had this strange proclivity, I felt relieved when I was hit. The fellow who hit me was named Kyōsu; he was an exceptional fellow of imposing force.

Katō continued to explain why he thought the beating was important in emptying him of what he referred to as his tendency to "look down on others." He said he often thanked Kyōsu for being responsible for his change.

Another reason Katō valued the fierce intensity of this rōhatsu sesshin was its effect on the new breed of intellectual monks. Many young monks had attended university, and Katō felt that, like himself when he was younger, they depended too much on intellectual processes in their practice. He felt the rough treatment at rohatsu helped shake these "philosopher monks" out of their tendency to try to think their way through practice.

> In the zendō, the assistant roshi would tell you to go to dokusan. You'd be sitting and he'd say, "Go to dokusan." When you did, there would be five or six assistants waiting at the garden. "What are you doing hanging around here?" they'd say. "Does it make any sense to flounder around in front of Roshi? Go back and sit resolutely. Go back to the zendō and sit." Then you'd go back to the zendō and you'd get yelled at by the assistant roshi and thrown out. So you'd collect yourself and try again, and once again you'd be greeted by, "What the hell are you doing here?" Such treatment is a form of violence. If it were one or two guys it wouldn't be so bad, but there were four or five, some with judo black belts. In the end you were desperate, and it no longer mattered how threatening they were or how much of a beating you took. You had no choice.
>
> You didn't see this kind of behavior in other zendōs. Not in Kyoto, not even in Shōgenji, the other "devil" monastery. At Shōgenji, they'd drag you out of the zendō. Those who didn't want to leave would be forcefully pushed out. They'd cling to something in the room and refuse to leave and a bunch of senior monks would come and drag them out. And you weren't allowed to go outside the main gate, so eventually you'd make your way to dokusan. That was the extent of the discipline. That is the way students were trained in all monasteries. But in Bairinji it was different. If they just said sit, I would have sat no matter how long, but they squeezed you from both sides. On one side they said go and on the other side they said don't go. It was impossible.

Katō goes on to say how if you were new to the monastery, in your first or second year, you really felt that the monks were devils, but in the bath after sesshin these same devils scrubbed your back and rubbed you down, praising you for practicing hard and later serving you rice gruel. You'd forget the anger you had for them. He added that he realized this kind of rough treatment was wrong, but he felt that humans who didn't have to bear the bitter with the sweet didn't really develop fully: "People today say that this kind of violence is unnecessary, that ways resembling those of the military should be abolished. They argue that we should acquire understanding peacefully. But it never happens [solely] that way. In order to reach people with different backgrounds and different living situations, you need both."

There are monasteries where such harassment and even violence is a smoke screen hiding a lack of genuine understanding. I was allowed to sit sesshin in a large Rinzai monastery in Kyoto a few years ago where I was certain that the expression of violence was an indication of a lack of true religious feeling on the part of the monks. I witnessed a young monk who couldn't stay awake and whose nervousness resulted in many errors of temple protocol get smacked around by senior monks whose intention, no doubt, was to discipline him. What struck me, however, was the anger these monks displayed and their lack of awareness that this young man was physically and emotionally weak and was unlikely to learn from such treatment.

I met the teacher, who was kind enough to allow me to participate in the session even though I was an outsider, after the sesshin was over and presented my observations to him, being careful not to be accusatory, which would certainly have been counterproductive. He explained to me that there will inevitably be some rough play when the tension of sesshin starts getting to the participants, but that the intention was to teach the new monks, and that severe methods were only for the purpose of furthering that goal. I then asked if it were proper for a head monk to jump in the air and throw a kick at the chest of a novice who was nodding. His expression changed dramatically. He quickly responded that there were prescribed methods for waking a nodding student and that a flying kick was certainly not one of them. I felt certain from the look on his face that he was going to confront the head monk of that training period, and I hoped it would have an effect.

Katō became a disciple of Kōmushitsu, a small, subdued man, who in Katō's words "was skillful at obsequious bowing." Kōmushitsu appeared the antithesis of his teacher, Sanshōken, a tall, husky man with a jovial and dynamic personality. At first Katō was devastated at losing the chance to study with Sanshōken, and he contemplated leaving Bairinji. But he stayed on, and after studying with Kōmushitsu he was to conclude that this man who first appeared to him "insignificant" was "the perfect teacher for me."

Though, as mentioned previously, inka shōmei, or "certification," is thought of in America as proof of the attainment of enlightenment, it is given in Japan to legitimize a teacher's right to be in charge of a training monastery. At least that was the reason one received it at Bairinji. You had to complete your koan training to receive inka, but you didn't necessarily receive inka just because you completed that training.

Kōmushitsu never received inka shomei from his teacher. Sanshōken said there was no need to do so because he was nearby and could always testify as to Kōmushitsu's right to teach. Sanshōken had given inka to two other students who were teaching at other monasteries, but there were others who, though having completed their training with him, never received inka. He clearly didn't like the ceremony and avoided it when he could. When Sanshōken died, Kōmushitsu still hadn't received inka from the master and refused to continue teaching at Bairinji without this official certification. In order to rectify this situation, Mokurai Takeda, Zen master of Kenninji Monastery and recipient of one of the two inka shomei Sanshōken did bestow, performed the inka ceremony, passing it on to Kōmushitsu in order to keep him from leaving Bairinji.

Katō talked about the difficulty with inka—that some who receive it become complacent. He felt that if you were serious about practice, you would always be stretching yourself. "You know when you have the real inka," he wrote. "Another person can never really know whether you have experienced awakening. Roshi told me I have experienced it, but I know it's still incomplete. Inka means only that you've completed your koan training, and it is necessary, on a certain level, to certify this. But the most important thing is your feeling 'this is it,' the feeling of 'great peace,' which is the objective of Zen practice. If you receive inka and you don't feel the peace, it's meaningless."

Katō was quite clear about his own degree of attainment: it wasn't complete, he still had to train. But he also felt that those who thought they no longer needed to train were probably fooling themselves.

> Since I'm not much good at anything else, I've come this far professing the one road, "zazen, zazen." But I realize that death is right before me. Aware that things are still incomplete, I have to be vigilant and sit zazen. But however I look at it, I don't think much will happen. On the other hand, it's all right because whatever happens there's always some dissatisfaction. When you build a house, it's no good to make it without any gaps. You should always leave something unfinished. That's the way it is: "If it's full, it will spill over." It's the same with people. If you think you are complete, then there is nothing ahead except death.

Compared to his charismatic teacher Sanshōken, Kōmushitsu might be described as someone of no import. Once Katō made the decision to study under him, however, he had the opportunity to see his teacher's true worth and to appreciate what had previously appeared to him as the behavior of a man of little consequence.

Kōmushitsu was fastidious in the extreme. It was said that he would use every drop of water three times before pouring it out.

> When people wash their face they simply discard the water . . . but he [Kōmushitsu] was the kind of person who had a precise way in which

he wanted everything done. You rarely find people like him. He often talked about Dōgen Zenji, and I think he was perfectly in accord with the meritorious conduct of the ancients described in the "*Gyōji*" (Maintaining Practice) chapter of Dōgen's *Shōbōgenzō*. I was by his side all the time and I know him well: he wouldn't let a drop of water spill.

Katō described how Kōmushitsu used rags until they were reduced to shreds, employing them for different tasks at different stages of their deterioration; how he had a place for everything and knew immediately if something was missing; and how he noticed and commented on everything Katō did. Once he stopped Katō from sweeping away a spider's web because he said the spider was showing him its art.

Kōmushitsu never discarded anything that was at all useable. Katō quotes him as saying, "Every object has a life, and its true nature is to preserve its life."

I served as Kōmushitsu's attendant for a long time, assisting him in many ways. I felt veneration when I saw the care with which he did his work, but when you are by his side he can be quite annoying. It's not that he berated you, but you felt as though you were always being watched. When I started serving him, even spreading out futons was a demanding task. I would naturally spread them out my own way, and he would say, "I have my way, watch me," and he would start. "You spread the bottom futon [the one that serves as the mattress], then you fold it over again and cover it with the upper futon [the one that serves as the cover]. You shouldn't stand on the bottom futon." That's true. It's improper to stand on the futon of an esteemed person. He repeated, "You shouldn't step on it. If it were for me it wouldn't matter, but when you are preparing the bedding for a respected person, you should never stand on it. That's why you spread it out first, then fold it in half, then cover it with the upper futon, fold it and then spread both."

Katō goes on to describe Kōmushitsu's comments on his way of hanging a mosquito net, preparing pickles, and doing just about everything else: never scolding, just watching and then saying, "I have my way of doing it." He felt sorry for his teacher having to eat the same meager vegetarian fare day in and day out, and he went out and bought some fried tofu for a treat. But he could never mention to Kōmushitsu that he bought it; he'd have to tell him that someone came by and donated it to the temple. Even then he would get a lecture about how eating special foods at the monastery takes the joy out of eating outside when invited.

Though Kōmushitsu was quite talkative around his students, Katō told of how uncomfortable his teacher was when he went out to another temple for a big Buddhist ceremony and had to sit in the seat for esteemed guests. While all the other monks were a little tipsy from drinking and engaged in frivolous conversation, Kōmushitsu would turn to the alcove and practice zazen.

What impressed Katō most about his teacher was the way he seemed to have transcended the desires for name and fame. Even when he was the abbot of Bairinji, he lived simply. While his teacher was alive, he played the role of junior partner, taking care of all the details while Sanshōken carried out all the public business of the monastery. When Sanshōken was living in a retreat house, having retired from temple duties, Kōmushitsu attended to the monks, giving dokusan until nine in the evening and then going to care for his teacher. During the hot months he would massage and fan Sanshōken until he fell asleep. He did it, in Katō's words, "because filial piety was simply a part of him, without any feeling that he was doing something [special]."

Though Kōmushitsu was in charge of Bairinji, he refused to wear robes that designated that position as long as his teacher was alive. He felt that he was simply acting in his teacher's stead as a natural part of his service.

Katō had come to Bairinji having practiced with a number of Zen teachers, both Rinzai and Sōtō. None of them impressed him enough to encourage him to stay with them. Although some, like Sōen Shaku, may not have been right for him, a bigger part of the problem, as Kanryō pointed out to him, was his unwillingness to let go of his own ideas. Kanryō thought that a dynamic teacher like Sanshōken might help Katō recognize his own role in his unsuccessful search for a teacher and a suitable practice. It's quite possible that the dynamic Sanshōken might have disappointed Katō in the end; dynamism can pale with familiarity. Kōmushitsu, on the other hand, small and unimpressive as he appeared on first contact, had a depth that kept Katō reaching to try to understand. Katō needed this, and once he realized that fact, his real training began.

After four and a half years at Bairinji, Katō was put in charge of a temple near the monastery. For fifteen years he continued to meet with his teacher daily for dokusan.

At some time during this period Katō married. Unfortunately, he doesn't talk about why he got married, though that information would certainly provide us more insight into his life during this period. Marriage didn't disqualify him for appointment as abbot of Bairinji, but it certainly lowered the chances. According to his biographer Ryūmin Akizuki, some years later, despite his marriage, Katō was offered the position of abbot of Bairinji and of another large Rinzai monastery, Daisenji. He refused both.

Katō left Kyushu for Tokyo at the age of fifty-nine. A Bairinji friend, Shūgen Nakajima, invited him to live in what he was led to believe was a large temple.

Katō took his friend up on his offer. When he arrived, he found an old abandoned temple falling apart from years of neglect. With the help of his friend Kōdō Sawaki, the willingness to work, and the energy of one far younger than his years, Katō managed to rebuild the temple and survive there for the next thirty-five years.

> You ask why I came here. There is a temple nearby called Ryūjūin. The priest in charge of the temple was trained at Bairinji. He begged me to come here. I thought, "Well, maybe," and decided to try it. That was 1934. I was fifty-nine then.
> "There's this temple," he said, "waiting for you. You have nothing to worry about; just come." So I arrived with a look of confidence, and what do you think I found?—a temple abandoned for twenty years, in a terribly decayed and dilapidated state.

Katō contacted the parish requesting permission to live there, despite the condition of the place, and was refused. The parishioners thought that he, approaching sixty, was too old. He went to meet the parish representatives, displaying all the vigor of a twenty-year old: "'What are you talking about?' I said. 'I'm not ready for my funeral. I've been practicing up to now and my life is just beginning.' Hearing me out, they came to the conclusion that I 'still had a lot of spunk left.' And I responded, 'I have no choice.' After that they let me live at Tokuunin."

But Katō had no intention of being abbot: "When I went to the parish leaders I told them that I hate the thought of being in charge of the temple, and I didn't want to be an abbot. I said, 'But I'd like to plant plum trees throughout the temple grounds. I'll be abbot of the plum trees.'"

He farmed, planted trees, and practiced zazen. With time, a small group formed that practiced with him, and he conducted dokusan for them. He didn't like to lecture, however, so he didn't. His strength was in encouraging others to practice. Like his friend Sawaki, he had tremendous faith in the power of zazen. Of all the teachers featured in this book, he was most insistent on zazen's importance.

> I don't lecture because it has no effect. I don't know the first thing about lecturing. It's different for scholars and distinguished men such as Mumon Yamada. All I do is sit with you and carry the keisaku stick. I don't get tired because this is the only thing I know.
> I constantly say that everything is the same; nothing is separate. I mean all is one. Of course this is just theory. Many things appear—loss and gain, for example—but still, if you reflect that originally they were one, you won't become attached. Even when someone slights you, if

> you reflect on your relationship with others being originally one, you will go to the heart of the matter. But no matter how much you understand the reasoning, if you haven't grasped it with your *gut,* you can't respond properly. If you practice Zen wholeheartedly you will get it; you must cultivate the energy to erase the illusion [of duality]. You approach Zen through objects; by objects I mean form and practice.

Katō's philosophy is simple: everything is originally one. Returning to that understanding is, for him, "right living." The method to reaching that understanding is zazen. He practiced zazen for over sixty years and he did not feel deceived.

> Even three or five minutes [of zazen] done each morning will become a habit. It will feel good. When you wash your hands after going to the toilet, it feels good, doesn't it? If you don't wash, it doesn't feel good.... When I don't do zazen it doesn't feel right. That's the feeling I'd like you to develop. It's not very difficult.
>
> If you forget to practice, it's like a person forgetting who he is, like a person forgetting his self-esteem or his value. If you see yourself as a person who has within himself the invaluable power to move the world, you won't go wrong. When you don't believe in yourself, you feel like a lowly insect.
>
> Through zazen, you will realize your own worth. The Buddha referred to those who have accomplished this as "perfect personalities," and they are.

Katō's emphasis on concentrating your energy in the *tanden* (lower abdomen), is particularly characteristic of his Rinzai Zen study. Sawaki talks about putting your mind in the tanden, but not with the same emphasis as Katō. Uchiyama and Yokoyama, Sawaki's chief disciples, say little if anything about it.

> The lower abdomen is the center of all the nerves. The abdomen controls the entire body. Zazen maintains the posture in which [energy] is concentrated in the lower abdomen. When you sit, your energy goes to the abdomen and controls the entire body. When you think trivial thoughts, your energy goes to your head. When you concentrate it in your lower abdomen, the energy doesn't fragment—it all becomes one, *the whole universe settles there.* You are one with the world; your source is the same as that of heaven and earth, and your body is the body of all things. The object of Buddhism is to perfect the person, the body-

mind. There is no Buddha outside of the human being, which means it [Buddhism] perfects the universe.

For a long time after Katō completed his own intensive training at Bairinji, he worked with a few students who had considerable monastic experience. Some of them were sent to him from Bairinji to spend a few years honing their practice. He seems to have kept a low profile for two reasons: he was very serious about training, and he was basically a shy man. But his reclusive nature is the one thing for which he expressed regret, saying that if he could do it over again he would shout zazen from the rooftops and announce it over the airwaves.

> When I think about my time spent here, I realize that I have failed. I've blundered for a long time. Though I've connected with some people like Yanase, I haven't allowed the general public to approach me.[5] I didn't have time for them. Among the people who visited, there were those who were suitable to this place and I naturally related to that special few, ignoring the general public. That's not what Buddhism is about. I realize that I should have been relating to the local farmers and other parishioners after all. Now when I tell those people, "Zazen is good for you, come sit with me," nobody comes. They think it's something very difficult.
>
> I have to work hard to get people of our country to practice zazen. That is my cherished wish now.
>
> When I ask kids after they've practiced zazen what they feel, they say they feel good. That's because their minds are working. It's best with children. With young children I make it like a game. With seven- and eight-year olds, when I take one thing from a group of objects and ask them to guess which one I've picked, they usually guess correctly. Adults, on the other hand, can't, because of their delusions. If they were to empty their minds, they would guess correctly without thinking.

Sit with your legs crossed, back straight, and breathe deeply while pushing your lower abdomen out—that would probably be how Katō would advise someone to sit in zazen. Katō was known for his protruding lower abdomen, which was especially prominent because he had a small, thin physique. His many years of putting a slight pressure in this area during zazen caused the protrusion. He was proud of his

---

[5] Yanase was one of Katō's two dharma heirs.

stomach, but when he watched sumo wrestlers, huge men with enormous bellies, he said that he had met his match.

These physical constraints in the zazen posture, Katō said, allow you to return to your original state. Infants, he continued, naturally breathe deeply from the lower abdomen. As they grow, bad habits develop. Posture starts to droop and abdominal breathing gives way to thoracic (chest) breathing. Zazen is training to return to your natural state. Breaking habits developed over many years requires great effort, but, according to Katō, the effort is well worth it. He attributed his long life to the practice of zazen.

Katō talked about being round shouldered when he started sitting and having straightened up as a result of zazen. But, he said, proper posture and correct breathing are not enough. If effort is not made to remain aware of yourself and your environment—that is, if you sit up straight but in a mental fog—your zazen has no meaning. There are people, he insisted, who are in perfect accord with the zazen state who have never practiced formal zazen. This, he claimed is because zazen is not anything unusual. It is the natural, inherent path of wisdom.

Katō was ninety-four when he made these reflections. Though they are remarkably clear for a man of his age, some of his statements are rather extreme. He suggested, for example, that zazen be a required subject in schools from kindergarten through university, and that no one be graduated unless they had completed the zazen requirement.

When responding to Akizuki's question about death, Katō said that when he felt death near he planned to sit and refrain from eating. At that time, he added, he would like someone to put a sign outside the entrance of the zendō with the words, "Still Practicing."

According to Akizuki, on January 31, 1971, Katō fell over and died while in the seated posture. He was ninety-six years old.

○

Kōzan Katō, farmer monk and teacher of Zen masters of some of the largest monasteries in Japan, spent the last three decades of his life in a small temple in a suburb of Tokyo. He taught a small group of students, raised a family, planted trees, farmed, and drank tea with his neighbors.

To his neighbors he was the wise, affectionate priest of Tokuunin, the poor temple down the road. To a small circle of monks who had some contact with Bairinji, he was an important teacher from the Bairinji lineage. To Kōdō Sawaki he was a respected friend and companion in zazen.

He struggled in poverty to feed his family and continue his life as a Buddhist practitioner, but his joy was infectious. He said that as he looked back on his life he realized that his most trying times were the best. He had few regrets.

"When it's hot," he said, "go outside and work as hard as you can. Then go into your house and practice zazen. The cool breeze you will feel is not a result of any man-made invention [like a fan]. The coolness will naturally come from the depth of your belly. It will be as if you entered a cool room. That's the way you have to approach hardship. If you endure your suffering, it will be the seed of joy."

Despite Katō's praise for the value of the severe training he went through and the spare life he chose for himself, he was neither dogmatic nor impractical. One of his students relates the following encounter with Katō some days before the Roshi's death. A neighbor of this student made honey for a living. Receiving some of the honey, he went to Tokuunin to share it with his teacher. He found Katō lying down. After the usual greeting, Katō said to him, "I'm going on an extended fast." When asked why, Katō responded, "I've always wanted to get everyone in this country to practice zazen. I thought that if I fasted, it might even reach the ears of the emperor, eventually having the benefit of urging everyone to do zazen." The student then said, "You have many advanced disciples. They can spread the teaching of the Way. Leave it to them and today try some of this honey I've brought."

The Roshi sat up and said, "Good point," and he started to lick the honey.

It was Katō's ability not only to laugh in the face of adversity but also to see true value in all experiences that gave him a joyous aura that drew so many to him. His joyous presence and his positive worldview blasted away all doubts and sadness. Whether this power he exercised was a result of zazen or not, it made those who met him want to try the practice he recommended so enthusiastically and find out for themselves.

4 MOTOKO IKEBE

THE SECOND WAVE OF WESTERNERS

When I first arrived at Gentaku, there were four Canadian nuns, disciples of a guru named Anandabodhi. They didn't stay very long but their presence was strongly felt. It wasn't until they left that we became aware of the relative quiet that existed before their arrival. Their constant buzz of energy reminded me of the chirping of the cicada announcing the beginning of summer—you aren't aware of the noise those little insects make until they miraculously stop in unison.

A few of us were gathered in an apartment one day talking and relaxing when Jauna, one of the Anandabodhi nuns, came in and announced her idea of inviting a Tokyo-based Taichi teacher to Gentaku to hold classes for those interested. Most of us weren't interested, but the idea seemed fine until her next remark: she said she thought the Antaiji zendō would be a great place for the classes, and that since Taichi was also a kind of meditation the Roshi would probably agree. That's when many of us found ourselves staring at the floor and wishing that the subject had never been brought up. Jauna sensed the apprehension in the room and asked what the problem was.

"I don't think it's such a good idea," someone muttered.

"Why not?" Jauna responded with a puzzled look on her face.

Some of us remained with our eyes glued to the floor while others just stared in disbelief. We may not have been at Antaiji very long, but we were there long enough to have learned something of our host culture. To request something that was probably unacceptable was to put the other person in a difficult position, especially if he was Japanese and you were not. We were quickly adopting Japanese attitudes, to which Jauna was oblivious. She was losing patience.

"Steve, will you come with me to the Roshi's room and interpret? I want to ask him for permission to use the zendō for the classes."

Steve looked down again, mumbling a vague refusal.

"Tom, what about you?" Jauna wasn't giving up that easily.

"I don't think so," Tom said quietly.

"Well I don't see what the big deal is. It is a meditation, isn't it?"

I can't remember exactly how this ended, but I think there was some more quiet and then someone brought up a new topic. Jauna was flabbergasted by the reception her suggestion received, and when we broke up she went to the young monk Ippei, with whom she was friendly, and asked him to interpret for her. Uchiyama quickly said no and that was the end of the Taichi incident. The cultural divide seemed greater between Jauna and the rest of us than between the Japanese and us.

Though this incident took place early in the years of the encounter between Antaiji and the West, it pointed to a gradual shift in outlook among the Western students who came to practice there. Younger people were coming to the neighborhood, many of them directly from the United States or Europe. They had been teenagers in the sixties, when Zen Buddhism had begun to become more familiar in the West, and the word "Zen" had become synonymous with meditation. Thanks to works like Aldous Huxley's *Perennial Philosophy*, the idea that all religions lead to the same end was also becoming an assumption of the sixties revolution that had shaped their attitudes—though it had certainly not shaped the attitudes of Japanese Zen monks at this time.

Though the Japanese did not share a belief in the commonalty of all religious goals, and by extension, the commonalty of all meditation, this difference in attitudes between them and their Western students did not cause any great disturbance. Another new Western idea— gender equality—certainly did, however. It challenged deep-rooted Japanese cultural traditions and practices, which are usually far more powerful than new philosophies and at the same time far more nuanced. As more men and women who had been raised in relatively equalitarian societies arrived at Gentaku, they simply assumed that women could participate equally in all activates. Though the Japanese experienced some initial discomfort when faced with these assumptions, at the same time it no doubt was a learning experience for them. More Western women came to sit at Antaiji, and they behaved much like the Western men. Many of them were studying Japanese, and they practiced their new language with the monks; this gave the monks an opportunity to broaden their horizons as well and reconsider, if not revise, the views of women they had grown up with.

The new consciousness evolving at Antaiji was nurtured by three factors: Western women seeking to communicate respectfully with the monks; a new breed of monk, interested in learning more about the world outside the Zen monastery; and an abbot whose gentle presence and democratic vision made Antaiji uncharacteristically open for a Zen temple.

In 1973, I was living on the other end of Kyoto from Antaiji. I spent less time around Gentaku when nothing particular was going on at the temple. I returned to the neighborhood before and after sesshins, Sunday zazen meetings, and lectures by Uchiyama. When I did drop into Tsuchihashisō, I got to know a new group of people. Owen, who lived in Greg's old apartment, was a big burly fellow from Omaha. He had thick glasses, red hair, and was as gentle as a teddy bear. He had just graduated from Colgate University with a major in Asian Studies and spoke some Japanese. Of our first encounter, all I can remember is his question, "Is it possible to sail from Kyoto to Kameoka in an inner tube?" I wondered whether this was some sort of koan. I told him that I had never thought about it, but I've also never forgotten it.

Molly lived two apartments down from Owen. She was twenty-two, a graduate in psychology, and had come to Japan to study Zen. She seemed to have a natural talent for learning languages, and she soon became fluent in Japanese. Molly made friends easily wherever she went, and she went everywhere. She traveled to India to a vipasana retreat, and soon after she returned, Darrel and Jennifer showed up at Tsuchihashisō from India on Molly's recommendation. They took the apartment between Molly and Owen. Molly's trip to Bangladesh resulted in two Bangladeshi brothers living and studying in Japan under her sponsorship.

Owen, Molly, Darrel, and Jennifer had fresh youthful energy that did not threaten the monks; some began to frequent their apartments, apparently enjoying the social freedom they felt there.

I dropped in Owen's apartment one day to find Owen, Molly, Jennifer, and some others and a few monks having tea. They were laughing and having a fun time. Two of the monks were laughing with everyone else but saying little. A third, Kōjō, was talking and laughing and appeared to be right at home. He was a round-faced, laughing Buddha type and was on the road to returning to lay life, whether he was aware of it at the time or not.

Kōjō had just graduated from Ryūkoku University. When someone told him that I was a teacher at Ryūkoku, he turned to me with his jaw hanging down.

"You teach at Ryūkoku?" he said laughing.

"Yes."

"A Ryūkoku teacher!" he repeated and continued laughing.

We were all hippies in the eyes of the monks. He was startled and confused to learn that this particular hippie before him was not only a university teacher but also taught at his alma mater! He just kept repeating, "A Ryūkoku teacher!" and laughing. Though surprised, he was prepared to accept this revelation. Here was a new brand of monk, a joy to behold.

Hilde was a young Swedish woman whom I'd met on the bus in downtown Kyoto. She had been studying pottery in Sweden. She visited Japan with her brother and father, and when they decided to return to Sweden she chose to stay in Japan. She was nineteen then. I don't remember mentioning Antaiji to her during our conversation on the bus, but the next time I visited Tsuchihashisō she was living there in the apartment under Jennifer and Darrel. Hilde had blond frizzy hair, very blue eyes, and a sparkling smile. She went regularly to sit at Antaiji, causing quite a stir among the monks, though she seemed unaware of it. Many of the monks were attracted to her, but only one, Kōjō, would admit it. The others satisfied their suppressed desires by counseling Kōjō and reprimanding him for inaction. He and Hilde did eventually go places together, and Hilde clearly enjoyed the attention she received from the monks at Antaiji, but no serious relationship developed from this innocent infatuation.

Relationships did start to grow at this point, the need to learn English acting as a catalyst for the monks. One of them, Kōshi, was studying English in preparation for his trip to the United States. After he left for the United States, two more monks, Shōhaku and Eishin, began English classes with the intention of eventually joining Kōshi. Until now, the Westerners, who had come to Japan with the sole purpose of studying Zen, were the ones interested in forming relationships with the monks; now at least some of the monks had a need to reach out to the Westerners. I saw an illustration of this change at a party: Kōshi, a conservative Kyoto resident and a serious monk, doing the twist amidst a group of inebriated foreigners. Having been chosen to support the group in Massachusetts, he was apparently determined to understand the culture in which he would soon be living.

Kōjō, too, began to study English. By that time Jennifer and Darrel had split up, and Jennifer started to teach Kōjō English. I spent very little time at Tsuchihashisō then, and this affair appeared to move much faster than I realized. I remember seeing Kōjō at Tsuchihachisō once, at an art show with Hilde another time, and then in a comic role in one of our last plays. The next I remember, he had entered a relationship with Jennifer and left the temple.

Kōjō was the oldest child in a family that owned a rice store, and he was expected to take over the family business. During his university days he read some of the works of Dōgen, founder of the Sōtō Zen Sect, and attended Uchiyama's lectures at Antaiji. He also joined the Antaiji community for zazen. I'm sure that the influence of these new ideas he learned from Dōgen and Uchiyama made him question the meaning of spending his life running the family rice store. Kōjō decided to become a monk.

When Kōjō joined Antaiji, he was, in a certain sense, becoming a part of a new family. I wonder if he found the new pressures of temple life—obeying one's superiors and behaving in ways Zen monks were expected to behave—similar to the pressures of taking over a family business, pressures that brought him to Antaiji in the first place. Our group of Westerners who practiced zazen but managed to avoid many of the pressures of Japanese communal life must have been extremely attractive to the novice monk. His involvement with the Westerner community led to his meeting Jennifer, and their subsequent relationship made remaining at Antaiji impossible.

Japanese Zen monks often marry, and celibacy is not a precept that many of them adhere to, but they are expected to refrain from marriage during the time they are training at a monastery. Uchiyama wanted his monks to train for ten years at Antaiji, and he expected them to refrain from relationships with women during that time.

Uchiyama talked about his own initiation into temple life and how he, too, wanted to get away from the constraints of Japanese society. He said that at thirty his wife died and he felt like his life was falling apart. On his father's recommendation he went to practice at a Zen temple. He stayed for the three-year period he had agreed on with his father, but when the time was up and he tried to return home his father said, "Bodhidharma sat for nine years," and chased him back to the temple. After ten years, he said, he saw the value of zazen in his life and decided to stay on for another ten years. Uchiyama's personal experience was at least partly responsible for his emphasis on practicing for ten years before drawing any conclusions about the effects of zazen.

Of all the factors that give Antaiji its special flavor, nothing stands out more than the unique nature of its abbot. Uchiyama had been married twice before he became a monk, and he entered the Buddhist order at a time when he felt his personal life was falling apart. He was both physically and emotionally frail. His teacher, Sawaki Roshi, was an imposing figure, and the contrast must have been intimidating to the young, fragile Uchiyama. I've heard him repeat in dozens of lectures: "When

I started to practice under Sawaki Roshi, I thought it would make me strong and brave like him. But here I am thirty years later and I'm still a wimp." Uchiyama emphasized that "zazen will not make you a different person." After all his practice he remained frail and soft spoken, and though he did not appear to be a wimp by any standard, his softness and honesty were far more appealing to those of us with a sixties mindset than the "war-hero ruggedness" Sawaki exemplified.

The attraction of Uchiyama's approach not only drew Westerners, particularly Western women, to Antaiji but also attracted Japanese women to practice there. I am not saying that he was a ladies' man but rather that he allowed people who normally felt unwelcome in the extremely male-dominated Zen environment to feel at ease in his temple.

Antaiji did not follow the military model that most training temples adopted. Though there was a degree of masculine posturing there, too, it was more a reflection of traditional Japanese male attitudes—exemplified at Antaiji by the head monk, Kōhō. But it was the Roshi who really set the tone at Antaiji, and he did not, by any stretch of the imagination, exude male domination. While Japan has an ancient warrior tradition that glorifies dominance, aggression, and violence, it also has a tradition that prizes refined beauty, compassion, and emotional sensitivity. Zen culture contains both elements, and the military tradition often seems to dominate at training temples. At Antaiji, however, one perceived both traditions, the masculine and the feminine, coexisting. The presence of a nun living there full-time, an unusual occurrence at a Zen temple, exemplified this special character of Antaiji.

Jōshin was about the same age as Uchiyama. She too was a disciple of Sawaki, and she joined Uchiyama at the time of Sawaki's death, when Uchiyama took over as abbot of Antaiji. Though she had a strong will and in some ways resembled the women from the old samurai clans who fought alongside their husbands, her outward behavior was that of a soft, beautiful flower. Jōshin provided another dimension to this unusual temple. She embodied the devotional aspect of the religious life, an aspect that interested the second wave of Westerners more than the first. Jōshin cooked for the sesshins when I first arrived at Antaiji and continued doing so for most of the time Uchiyama was abbot. She was already sixty when I began living there, and it was starting to become difficult for her to carry the big tubs of rice, which grew heavier each year with the increasing number of people participating in sesshin. She was so inconspicuous throughout sesshin that if Uchiyama hadn't turned to her during the final ritual, bowing and thanking her for her work, we wouldn't have known that she had been in the kitchen cooking and cleaning up throughout the five days. She traveled quite a bit between sesshins, but returned, without fail, each month to cook and at other times to sew surplices for the monks and to make sitting cushions (*zafu*) for the meditation hall.

On the surface, Jōshin was accommodating and easygoing. In fact, she preferred to remain anonymous, doing her work quietly and diligently. But when it came to defining what her work should be in the larger sense, she gave no quarter. She did whatever was needed at Antaiji with the smile of one who loved her work, but the decision to be at Antaiji in the first place was without a doubt hers. The decision to be a Sōtō Zen nun under Sawaki Roshi, too, was clearly hers.

Jōshin was missing part of her pinkie on her right hand. She started her Buddhist practice sitting in a temple under the charge of Harada Roshi, a teacher well known in the West thanks to Philip Kapleau. Harada taught a Zen that appeared to be a blend of Rinzai and Sōtō but was distinct from either school. Whatever kind of Zen it was, it was certainly nothing like the teachings of Sawaki. At some point early in her practice, perhaps at her first sesshin, Jōshin broke through her first kōan and was recognized as having had a kenshō experience. As with Kōzan Katō before her, this unusually early kenshō made Jōshin doubt her teacher and the whole system of kōan practice as well. She left Harada and studied under a Sōtō Zen teacher named Ekō Hashimoto. During her stay with Hashimoto, Jōshin came in contact with Sawaki. I believe that Jōshin had taken formal ordination under Hashimoto; when she met Sawaki and decided that he was the teacher for her, she found herself in a difficult situation. She wasn't going to let formalities prevent her from choosing a mentor who she regarded as a true Dharma master. In the world of Japanese Zen Buddhism of the twentieth century, it was not as easy to leave one teacher for another as it may have been in antiquity (and even then we only know about the monks who were quite determined)—nor as easy as many American Zen Buddhists seem to find it. But Jōshin was determined, and she made up her mind to show her resolve by cutting off part of her little finger, an act more typically committed by Japanese gangsters to prove their loyalty to their boss.

This little powerhouse of a nun was also the only person who would stand up to Kōhō, the head monk at Antaiji. In the presence of Uchiyama, who always showed her respect, Jōshin was sweet, quiet, and reverent. Kōhō, the dynamic young head monk, inspired different behavior from Jōshin. He had a fierce temper and could be quite intimidating. I know of nobody who, once experiencing his wrath, repeated the action that caused it. Jōshin, however, had a reputation for standing her ground. Sawaki once asked her to leave the temple, and she responded by going into the back room and sitting in zazen for two days until Sawaki relented. So when Kōhō talked roughly to her, she confronted him fearlessly: "I know everybody is afraid of you," she would say, "but I'm not." Faced with this indomitable little woman almost twice his age, even Kōhō could do nothing other than mutter under his breath and leave; I suspect he secretly respected her for standing up to him.

Molly was typical of the second wave of Westerners in Kyoto who came to practice Zen but saw Zen as one expression of a universal truth that manifested itself in many forms. Before she was to leave Kyoto for good in 1976, along with having attended the vipassana retreat in India, she spent a winter in the Zen monastery of Songgwang-sa in South Korea. It was also Molly who arranged for my meeting with Motoko Ikebe. While many of us found it difficult enough just to make a living, have a personal life, and maintain a steady practice, Molly was reaching out to other teachers and taking part in other practices in addition to coming to Antaiji for regular sesshins.

Molly told me of a Japanese woman who taught Zen meditation and did astrological readings. A group of the Gentaku Westerners were going to meet her, and Molly asked if Hiroko and I would like to join them and perhaps help with the interpretation of Ikebe Sensei's talk. I was interested, and when I mentioned it to Hiroko, she was excited to meet a woman who taught in what appeared to her to be an exclusively male domain. Hiroko had been studying a a traditional Japanese style of painting called Nihonga, and her interest intensified when she heard that Ikebe had been a Nihonga painter too. To this day I don't know how Molly and the others living in Gentaku came to hear of Ikebe, though she had taken lay ordination some years before under Uchiyama at Antaiji; but it is not surprising to me that a female teacher should appear at this time in the group's history.

Hiroko and I were living on the other side of town, so we met the rest of the group at Kyoto Station. The plan was to take the train to Kameoka, about twenty kilometers north of the city, to be picked up and taken from there to Ikebe Sensei's house. As with many of these "cross-cultural" affairs, communication was less than ideal. The fact that there would be eight Westerners coming was probably not clearly indicated to Ikebe Sensei; in fact the number may not have been known by the person from our side who arranged the meeting. When we arrived at the station there was one car to pick us up and it was clear that it would require two trips to transport us all. Ikebe's house was about a half an hour's ride from the Kameoka station so it took about an hour and a half to get us all there.

MOTOKO IKEBE SENSEI

We made our way over small country roads crowded with tiny houses, some old and traditional, others like oversized matchboxes. Nakagawa, a disciple of Ikebe, was our driver, and she took us through the narrow streets like a New York cab driver. She was a very masculine woman with a husky build, her hair in a bun, and a stoic expression. She didn't say a word the entire trip. As we approached Ikebe's, the number of roadside houses grew fewer and the modern, prefabricated type disappeared altogether. Ikebe lived in an old, traditional wooden cottage that was rather small and not very sturdy looking. It was situated halfway up a hill, with a creek flowing behind it. The first load of foreigners were standing in front of the house when we arrived, and next to them stood Shūko, a middle-aged nun who was Ikebe's adopted daughter. Shūko welcomed us in. If they were surprised at our numbers, they concealed it.

Ikebe, a frail woman of about seventy-five, was elegantly but simply dressed in a brown kimono. She wore large rimless glasses and her hair was neatly combed back. Though she lived very modestly, her grace gave her the look of one who was brought up in a cultured environment. She sat in formal Japanese style, her back remarkably straight for a woman of her age. We all bowed to her, and she welcomed us to her home with a bow in return. I didn't see Nakagawa again until we were ready to leave and she drove her car to the front of the house to pick us up.

Shūko served us tea.

Though meeting a teacher in Japan for the first time can be a bit awkward, Ikebe's warm manner soon put us at ease. She asked each of us our date of birth and wrote them down in her notebook, which she then put aside. She started to talk. Though I didn't take notes and I am left with only vague recollections of the details, my impressions of that meeting are still vivid. The general subject was Buddhism and the importance of zazen. She talked about how she and her husband had come to that house about thirty-five years ago with a small amount of money and a desire to be closer to nature and to live off the land as much as possible. It was clear from her constant references that her husband, who had died in his sixtieth year some twenty-five years before, was her teacher as well as her husband. He had either studied with Sawaki or read some of his writing and through that contact learned about zazen. At some point, he started to sit zazen, and under his influence, she, too, began to sit.

The impressions that stand out as I reflect back on that day are how poised she was and how simple and penetrating was her description of zazen. "Zazen," she said, "is sitting upright and letting delusions be." Not a particularly unique description and one I'd probably heard and read many times before, yet it felt as if I'd finally been introduced to zazen. Uchiyama had used the phrase "letting go of your thoughts" countless times, yet I never felt his words as powerfully as Ikebe's "letting delusion be." The way she sat up straight and spoke from a calm, meditative center allowed me to listen without resistance. I realize now that much of the calm, meditative feeling she imparted was the product of the upbringing of women of her class during early twentieth-century Japan, but that was only part of the story. Ikebe's faith in the practice was strong; this I was to learn again and again as I returned to see her many times

Encounters with Ikebe were different than those with other Japanese Zen teachers. Her interest in spirituality was quite broad in scope. The very things that I found difficult to tolerate in many of my contemporaries—equating Zen with vegetarianism, macrobiotics, Taichi, and everything under the sun related to the East and to mysticism—I found intriguing in a Zen teacher.

Ikebe was a practitioner of macrobiotics, a vegetarian, and an astrologer. At some time in her life she had studied and practiced Christianity, and the concept of Christian love was recognizable in her Zen talks. Zazen was the practice she had come to recommend exclusively, though many people still came to her to have their astrological charts done. She believed that the best thing we could do for ourselves was to sit and let our delusions be, but that it was also helpful to be informed as to where our karmic tendencies were leading us. Though she preached zazen, when asked questions about astrological influences, her face would light up with an excitement she couldn't hide.

Ikebe talked for an hour or so and then answered our questions. We agreed to visit her again in a month. Nakagawa appeared when it was time for us to leave, shuttling us in two shifts to the Kameoka train station.

The highlight of our next visit was Ikebe's reading of our charts. The readings on the whole weren't very exciting, mostly telling of positive futures, the kind you might find in an astrology section of a newspaper. One, Hilde's chart, however, did stand out. Hilde, as I mentioned above, was the star at Antaiji, presenting many monks with a struggle for self-control. Though she was clearly interested in the practice and had come to Antaiji to learn zazen, she didn't hide her enthusiasm for men, either. She was disappointed in her encounters with Japanese men, who were usually strongly attracted to her but not looking for a long-term relationship with a Western girl. If the other women in our group were longing for male companions, they were not revealing it.

Ikebe knew nothing about any of us at that time, so it was interesting that only Hilde's chart made mention of the men in her life. According to Ikeba, there were a number of men in her future. One was described, oddly, as square headed. I was embarrassed to ask what square headed actually meant and, so translated it literally. Nobody questioned my translation so they were either satisfied with the description or, more likely, also too embarrassed to ask. Hilde had one question, though: she wanted to know if the square-headed guy was Japanese.

There were no more meetings scheduled with Ikebe, and none of the group expressed a desire for one, but I was sure I wanted to see her again. A couple of others in the group also went to see her individually. Ikebe had a small group of Japanese followers who met with her monthly for weekend sesshins and lectures. I joined them a few times for sesshins and visited her with Hiroko at other times.

Hiroko was moving away from Nihonga painting toward contemporary art. We were about to move to the United States and I wanted to visit Ikebe to say goodbye. Hiroko's initial interest in meeting Ikebe was to meet another woman artist. Now that neither of them painted in the Nihonga style, Hiroko was no longer drawn to Ikebe as an artist, but she was still attracted by Ikebe's expertise in the occult science of Chinese astrology. Though Ikebe remained interested in astrology, she rarely broached the subject with us, realizing no doubt that it was a suspect topic in the Zen world. Usually she said nothing about it unless we asked a specific question. In that respect this visit was different.

Soon after we arrived, Ikebe said she had just read her chart and, according to her reading, she would live another thirteen years. While she was telling us, she began to cry—I believe, because she had felt up until then that she didn't have long to live, and now she was given thirteen more years. I was skeptical about this revelation, gave it little credence, and thought no more of it—though I do recall my discomfort at her tears. She had always appeared a pillar of strength to me, and I wasn't prepared for this display of emotion.

I saw Ikebe twice more. I was only able to visit Japan during short breaks from my work in the United States. She had had a couple of strokes since I left Japan and tired easily. I made one trip back to Japan with my nine-month-old daughter, Nao. Acting the proud papa showing my child off to Sensei, Hiroko and I brought Nao, asleep in a basket, for Ikebe to see. Ikebe quickly checked Nao's tiny hands and told us about the future personality of our daughter. I shouldn't have been surprised that she read palms, but I was.

I lost contact with Ikebe. In the summer of 1997 I called the old phone number I had for her. Shūko answered the phone and informed me that Ikebe had died in 1989, thirteen years after that visit when she had told us of her chart reading.

Ikebe became known to the Japanese public through a small book she wrote for a series of books dealing with religious matters called *Mamizu Shin Sho* (New Writings of Pure Water) and published by Hakujusha Publishing Company. In her little book, Ikebe told the story of her life—or at least the parts of her life that she felt were significant to her spiritual development. The book was published in 1967, and two years later she participated in bimonthly meetings called *Mamizu Kai* (Pure Water Meetings). With the encouragement of enthusiastic followers, she coordinated zazen meetings and sesshins until her failing health made this impossible.

Zazen was for her the way to truly understand the meaning of the sutras and the way of the patriarchs. It was this faith and devotion to zazen that inspired me to tell her story. Her interests were much broader than the words of the patriarchs. She seemed to have read every spiritual text that was available to her. When she talked about the union of wisdom and love, which came with understanding the Way, it sounded more like the sermon of a Christian priest than of a Zen teacher. Though she rarely refers to it, she and her husband Kōhaku had been baptized in 1935. Another influence in her life was the writings of Vivakananda and the teachings of his teacher Ramakrishna. Together with her interest in natural healing, diet, and the occult, she seems as much a product of the sixties in America as any of the Westerners who came to meet her.

Most of the story I will recount comes from *Bi no Hate ni Atta Mono* (Something Beyond Beauty), the small book published by Hakujusha Publishing Company mentioned above; translations from *Ikiru Shisei o Motomete 1 & 2* (In Search of an Approach to Life), two books published by Ikebe's students after her death, or from the groups newsletter, *Nyoze*, are credited in footnotes.

> This world that appears in time and space, that continued from yesterday to today and continues through tomorrow and beyond—where in this chain does humankind live? Yesterday has passed, tomorrow hasn't come, and even now these moments in which I am speaking flow by each second. The Earth is turning and the content of my body-mind is changing continuously. In this place called the world, where the processes of creation and change are endlessly repeated, and where we never encounter the same situation twice, where events pile up, each a single occurrence called "now," I, like a speck of dust in a corner of this world watching it all, am here today as a result of whose will? Or is it all just by chance?

This opening paragraph of *Something Beyond Beauty* clearly demonstrates Ikebe's unique perspective. Like Katō, Sawaki, Yokoyama, and Uchiyama, she ends by telling us to just sit and drop our ideas; but unlike the others, she offers a distinctive and not necessarily Zen-style cosmology—a result, I believe, of the many other religious influences in her life.

Ikebe never tired of asking why we were put on earth—a question that occurs to most thoughtful people at some time in their intellectual development. At a very young age, Ikebe took an interest in painting, and her love of it eventually led her to art school. She graduated from Joshi Bijutsu Semmon Gakkō (Women's Art School, now Joshi Bijutsu Daigaku or Women's Art University). Most of the first chapter of *Something Beyond Beauty* is devoted to Ikebe's interest in art. As mentioned above, Ikebe's husband Kōhaku had a strong influence on his wife's religious development, but he also influenced her artistic interests. Kōhaku also aspired to be an artist and their initial connection was a result of their mutual interest in painting. Kōhaku, who had been studying Western painting, gave Motoko a book on Japanese art when he noticed her interest in it on her first visit to his studio. He was a precocious child with a very inquisitive mind. He talked with Motoko about beauty and God and his philosophy of nature. Long after his death, when she was a teacher in her own right, she often prefaced her insights with, "Ikebe (Kōhaku) used to say . . . ."

After their marriage, they went to Taiwan together, intending it to be a sketching trip. The beauty of the island and their fascination with the people drew them into the culture and they decided to stay there.

> The green of the *sōshi* trees, the red of the China rose under the deep blue sky; vivid nature brought to life by the unique squalls of the southern countries; the infinite quiet of bats flying in the spectacular sunset, the endless fields of pineapples and sugar cane, the horizon punctuated by boundless sea and sky, and the visual details—the people, the architecture, the water buffalo, the ducks and junks; and then, the women, each so attentive to her hair . . . our hearts were moved by something more than beauty . . . and what was to be a short stay ended in us settling there.

They went there as painters in search of beauty to sketch and ended up seeing a deeper beauty that they could never put to pencil and paper. They were captured by the simplicity of an indigenous people living close to nature in a way no longer possible in their sophisticated world.

From the beginning, their quest for beauty through art had a strong religious element and their contact with indigenous Taiwanese planted the seeds for their move into the Japanese countryside, where they attempted to live the lifestyle they had observed among the indigenous Taiwanese. In all their travels they carried the sutras of the Buddhist canon, the Holy Bible, and the Confucian Analects with them.

> Both of us earnestly desired to know through our art what created all existence on earth and what was behind this existence; we wanted to grasp this reality.

> These primitive peoples of the eastern shores and mountain regions had many things in their natural lives that we couldn't imitate and for which we were envious. Next to the need to eat is the desire to make things. These people sculpted, wove, and embroidered their living quarters, tools, and clothing with symbols of the love and power from their common surroundings. When the soul of man communicates with the soul of a block of wood, the result of the sculpted expression, the illusion created, has a flavor of simplicity that reveals a yearning of a heart that is naked. . . .

Ikebe doesn't mention the political realities of the times—the fact that Taiwan had been annexed by Japan—and I never thought to ask her how she felt about this. Whether she and her husband were blind to the political realities or chose to ignore them, they developed through this experience a belief that returning to a simpler style of living was essential for their spiritual growth.

They attempted to get Kōhaku's mother to stay with them in Taiwan, and when she refused their many requests, they decided to move back to Japan. Two years after returning to Japan, they joined a newly built local church. They wanted to accept the Christian faith but found they couldn't. Though they were told they wouldn't be saved through reason and enjoined to be "like innocent children and just believe," in the end they decided this was not the path for them.

Kōhaku spoke to Motoko of the times he went to a Zen temple in Kamakura to practice zazen in his youth. After they left the Christian church, he decided to make an attempt at seriously practicing zazen, and she joined him.

> Just about the time we started to practice zazen we found a booklet called *Zenke Yōjin Shū* (A Collection of Points to Watch in Zen) in an antique bookstore. After that we were guided in our practice by Dōgen Zenji's *Fukan Zazen Gi* (The Treatise on the Universal Recommendation of Zazen). While all kinds of thoughts came and went, we were pulled along by the feeling "We must sit" until the mind relaxed in a way I find difficult to explain. It was at this time that we became familiar with that very important book, Dōgen's *Shōbōgenzō*.

I translate the following account of a personal experience Ikebe had because it was important to her on her journey, but I do it with reservations because it is the kind of record that can encourage students to look to their teacher as some kind of "enlightened being." Ikebe, to a greater degree than any other teacher I describe, was treated by her students as a kind of higher being, which I am certain did not help the relationship between teacher and student. She had a reverent, even pious manner, and she regarded her students as though they were her children. Many of her disciples appeared to me to be quite dependent on her attentions. Accounts such as the one I translate below certainly promoted a worshipful attitude toward her.

> I believe it was 1938. The roses climbing up through the hedges were in full bloom, so it must have been around May. One evening when I was finally about to drop off to sleep—I was on the border between dream and reality— there was a faint sound of a shower. In this foggy state I thought to myself, "It's raining." In a few moments I felt a tightening in my chest and I became conscious of an obstruction to my breathing. There was nothing I could do, so I just observed it, and in the next moment it felt as if my breathing had stopped. Then I couldn't move my hands or my legs and I thought, "I must be dead."
>
> I started looking at death itself and feeling disinterestedly, "It's all right to die," looking down at—I have no other way of explaining it—this stretched-out body. The one looking down was the real self. Though it was clear that "I" existed, where was I? I wasn't anywhere. I wasn't anywhere, but I was. If I must explain, I would say that the "I" was the "seat of thought." That's what it felt like. Shall I call it a beautiful sky all aglow, or the quiet of sunlight reflecting on the sand at the bottom of a clear river?
>
> That's the way this self felt. At the same time all existence was beyond time and space; it was endless. "A human being is a splendid creature!" I thought. Even when dead I felt I could see my deathless self.
>
> At that moment I remembered the man I had left behind. When that thought occurred, I was instantly enclosed in my stiff body. And I thought, "Oh, this is attachment to the world. Truly, if you have a hair's tip of delusion, you won't be able to transcend time and space; leave worldly things to the world." And again, the splendor returned. Then I noticed that my heart began to beat again and I was again in my old body and there was the sound of heavy rain. Listening to the rain, I fell asleep. In the morning when I opened a window, the garden and the roses, soaked from the evening rain, were aglow.

Kōhaku and Motoko lived with Kōhaku's mother in Osaka after returning from Taiwan. Kōhaku was painting, but he didn't have any opportunities to display his work. Kōhaku and Motoko felt alienated in this situation, so when Kōhaku's mother moved back to Tokyo, the couple saw it as an opportunity to experiment with a simple life in the country. When they first moved to this area in 1940, they stayed in a woodcutter's shed, the only structure in the area.

> The mountain colors extended right up to our shed. The wet mountain air soaked the moss in the valley. You could hear the sounds of whispering pines though there was no wind. The beauty of the misty green of spring, the shining rainbow colors on the morning dew of summer, the flowing mist of autumn resembling a brush painting and the sleet of the long winter—not a day went by in this ever-changing natural panorama in which the same scene appeared twice.
>
> We cultivated a vegetable garden between the trees in the chestnut grove in spring, gathered pine needles and firewood in autumn—there was no better place for "working in fair weather, reading in rain," and keeping our minds in order.

When we arrived at Ikebe's house some thirty-five years after she and Kōhaku first moved in, its age was the only hint that it had once stood alone in that area: it was clearly the oldest house on the street and was, before my last visit to see her, torn down.

Ikebe's broad interests in the area of religion gave her talks a contemporary flavor. Unlike any other Japanese Zen teacher I know, she brought together ideas of God, love, compassion, meditation, and karma, synthesizing them into an integrated worldview. Ikebe's Christian background shows itself most clearly in her use of the word "God" (*kami*), suggesting the almighty God of Christianity rather than the Japanese *kami*. Another concept that is an integral part of her lectures and writings is that humans are the only animal with the power of reflection, which allows them to "reach God," or to become enlightened.

> There is no place where God is not. Sentient and non-sentient beings dwell in the life of God. In that respect human beings, birds, animals, insects, trees and grasses, and all things down to the tiniest pebbles are all equal. However, as the saying "Man is a thinking reed" indicates, human beings can think thoughts such as, "What am I? What is the meaning of life? Why was I born?" In this way, only humans can ask who they are—realizing that their heart-minds are reality. With this as a starter, they can know their relationship to God and to all other beings, and live their lives on this earth according to the will of God. It is because

of this and only this, that human beings can see the joy of awakening to the true existence.

Interestingly, Kōzan Katō expresses a very different view, regarding the human ability to think "sophisticated" thoughts as the reason for their delusion and their need to practice zazen.

> People who haven't awakened to the true nature haven't fulfilled their mission as humans. For other creatures, even insects, there is no need for awakening. They are nature as they are. Humans have fallen from their natural state because of delusion. So they awaken to their original nature that everything is one—to that original feeling. The mission of humans is to cease producing the waves [of thought] that have occurred up until now as a result of egotism. When that is done, a human being is born for the first time; that is the definition of a human being. Without that experience, no matter how renowned or eminent one is, no matter how great one's achievement in history is, one is after all a scoundrel, no different than the criminal [waiting to die] on the gallows. Without that [experience], no matter how respectable one may appear to be, everyone (excuse me for saying this), even the emperor, is a villain on the gallows. . . . So we have to do zazen. It's the most important thing in the life of a human being. Other animals are doing zazen naturally, so they don't have to make a special effort. Even insects, bugs, and worms are all doing zazen.
>
> Dogs and cats discriminate. They have true discrimination. Humans have deluded discrimination. Dogs, cats, and insects are hot when it is hot, cold when it is cold, but they don't discriminate in delusion as humans do. Humans, too, if they practice zazen, will naturally attain this state.[1]

One might well ask what besides their emphasis on zazen these two teachers have in common. Katō's training at Bairinji was physical and very strenuous. He had little time for extensive reading outside of the Zen literature. The atmosphere at Bairinji didn't encourage intellectual pursuits. Ikebe, on the other hand, tried to understand how to live through wide reading and her strong intuitive feeling of union with nature. Her struggle was much more intellectual than was Katō's. But like Katō her resolution was to give her all to zazen. Her faith in this practice was quite clear, as the following selections from her writings attest.

---

[1] *Zazen ni Ikiru*, 130–31.

○

There is no expression with deeper meaning than that of the word "just" in "just sitting." No matter what, throwing away the activity born of ignorant doings, you sit there, which means you are not being fooled. You stop delusion and sit.

"But most people can't do that," you say. That's because they hold onto delusion. "Delusions rise again. There's nothing I can do." You shake your head and shake off deluded thought, thinking, "Now it's fine." Then, "They've risen again." For an hour you keep shaking your head, but there's nothing you can do. Grasping delusions and trying to push them away, you think they will disappear. Just stop that, stop deluded thinking. Because you give these delusions your attention, they keep coming back.

Just cease deluded thinking and sit. The highest work a human being can do is to cease deluded thoughts. Zazen means just sitting. Don't be deluded. Don't think "good" don't think "bad." It is said, "Clarify life, clarify death, that is the most important meaning of Buddhism." Truly, just sit. . . . That's all there is.[2]

We've fallen into this existence because of our disregard for cause and effect, so we have to return to a place where we stop the causal mind. We have to transcend cause and effect. That is zazen. Zazen is ceasing to create karma. That's the reason we sit, isn't it? To stop creating karma and only that. Human beings can do nothing other than that. It's a lowly existence. We still think things like, "I'm a little more intelligent, or I'm a little luckier". . . but those thoughts amount to nothing. "I'm a little healthier" and so forth— none of that will do us any good, it's of no use whatsoever. Just sit. To actually travel the road of truth you only have to stop creating delusion. That's the only thing humans can do. Since it was humans who created delusions, all they have to do is stop. That's the only reason for sitting. Never mind what will happen next. This wholeness will act on us from within. Humans should do what they can, that is, cease creating delusion. Then awakening is already there, for anyone and everyone, without a doubt. It's written in the *Shushōji* [Dōgen's "Practice Enlightenment" chapter of the *Shōbōgenzō*] and in many other places.

---

[2] *Ikiru Shisei o Motomete*, 122–24.

So there is no need to worry, just cease creating delusion. "Ah, there it is again!" That thought too is delusion. If you give it attention, there is no limit to delusion. So quit creating delusions and just sit. Then when you face this way, which is your life, based on your practice, the posture in which you stop creating delusion is the sole true mind. Life's true wisdom is derived from this, from this work. It will arise from the true mind, undoubtedly.

"I've stopped creating delusion, why is it so trivial?" That thought too is delusion, isn't it? Consider it as when the brain stops. You feel gratitude, a feeling you've yearned for. You'll bow to everything, appreciate everything, and there you will continue your practice. But don't stain it by overdoing.[3] Act with a truly quiet mind of no thought.[4]

Since breath is the greatest aid to zazen, you must take special care with it. When you are attentive to your breath, you will naturally be attentive to your mind. Isn't that true? When you react to each encounter, your heart may start to pound, or it may tighten up. Or, if you are happy, for example, it may go pit-a-pat. It is constantly reacting this way as if it were being bullied [by each situation]. The heart works in conjunction with the lungs circulating the blood throughout the body. When the system is calm, blood circulates through the body smoothly. There are no lapses and you have good health. . . .

Start by counting your breath. You will eventually be doing it unconsciously. Count the number of breaths. When it becomes your own, you will no longer count. You will be able to breathe in a way that suits you. What's more, this state of mind in which you practice zazen will be expressed in your life. You will be able to breathe in this natural way in all states [of being].[5]

---

[3] This expression, *te aka o tsukeru* is equivalent (but not as clear) to Suzuki Shunryū's expression, "When you make some special effort to achieve something, some excessive quality, some extra element is involved in it. You should get rid of excessive things . . . [such as pride]." Shunryu Suzuki, *Zen Mind, Beginner's Mind* (New York and Tokyo: Weatherhill, 1970), 59.

[4] From a taped talk dated December 16, 1979.

[5] From a talk on November 23, 1979. Ikebe is explaining the meaning from a text on the Buddhist practice of breathing by Hiromasa Muraki, *Shakuson no Kokyūhō* (The Way of Breathing According to the Buddha), (Tokyo: Hakujusha, 1979).

When you say, "Another delusion! I can't do anything about it," you are giving these delusions wheels, aren't you? And when you say, "Why do they manifest? I'm so pitiful." You are holding onto this "pitiful self." There is no such thing, so just let go and there will be no problem. "If that's true" you say, "if it's okay to just sit there in a fog, wouldn't it be better to just go to sleep?" Waking up and sleeping are relative. If you're not sleeping, you are awake. We are not talking about problems of this world like waking or sleeping.

There is something unrelated to all that—something that continues to be awake through eternity, something that continues though you die. That's where you have to sit. There, your mind becomes perfectly clear and warm. You may think I mean warm in the sense of body temperature, but I don't. You may think that by perfectly clear I mean like the blue sky or a moonlit night. But examples like those are unnecessary. This transcends examples. The saint Ippen called it "quiescent no-mind." You must sit within "quiescent no-mind." The mind is not put to work. When it arises, you leave it as is. You let it be. It's because you pay attention to it that things arise one after the other ceaselessly. We call this [ceaseless arising] the demon because it stands in the way of our escaping from the three worlds.[6]

Now if you truly sit in quiescent no-mind, it's quite difficult to do it for an hour straight. You may say "I hear sounds." Since that is proof that your ears are working well, rejoice in it. If you can't hear anything when you are sitting, that would be reason for alarm. You may say, "My feet are becoming numb." If your legs don't become numb, something may really be wrong. Don't concern yourself with numbness, it can't be helped. Simply switch the position of your feet.

Just cease creating delusion; don't delude yourself. You have to sit in a manner in which delusion has no real relation to you. That's the way to sit.

When you were born, when you die, and in between, every breath is life-death. So you need not worry about it; there is no death. If you do zazen, you will realize this fact.[7]

---

[6] The worlds of unenlightened beings: the world of desire, the world of form, and the world of no-form.

[7] From a series entitled *Dō Tankyū no Shisei* (The Attitude of the Way Seeker), in *Nyōze*, issue 27, March 27, 1994.

From now on, throughout this year, sit resolutely. Sit through this year and the next. You should sit throughout your whole life.

Then when you realize "This is it" you won't continue accumulating karma. You won't pile up the three poisons. The three poisons are of this world. You will be throwing them away in zazen because you won't be holding on to them.

Holding on is the number-one fault. When you hold on you are not free. Then you won't even be able to have a cup of tea, you won't be able to hold the cup. You have to let go constantly. Hold on to something and the act of holding will soil it. Many times you hear people say, "I did it for him but he doesn't show any appreciation." The act is already soiled. You are doing it because you want favor bestowed upon you.

Since we are simply being allowed to do what we do, whatever happens is fine. If in an encounter I am acting in accord with my inner calling, there is no need to inquire into the results. We must treat each instance in this way, not giving attention to deluded thoughts, and since this "Mister Delusion" is just a lump of attachments, he will weaken, won't he? Then he will disappear for sure.

At any rate, if you advance in single-minded zazen here in this way, giving life to it, you will understand this feeling of gratitude. That's why you won't expect anything from anyone. . . . If you are expecting something, you have already adopted a greedy mind. When you yourself change, surely some people around you will be moved by that change. Your actions alone will be a great sermon. Sitting on a high seat, spreading the sleeves of your red robes, waving your hands, voice and body shaking, sermonizing, is not the real sermon. It is theater.

When your true self is practicing the activity of true mind, that is a great sermon. There is no other way. You may wonder, "What do I need to do to practice the activity of true mind?" You must realize more and more the "oneness." In zazen you will understand this oneness for a second or for a minute. It will accumulate.

Life is the universal creation. There is no more perfect work of art. That's how wonderful it is. . . . But past karma has made it necessary for me to suffer in this life. Karma is the form taken by effects of accumulation from causes.

Repentance is not saying, "I was wrong." When someone says, "I was wrong," it means nothing. Single-minded zazen, even for a minute, is the correct response. Sit true Tathagata Zen. . . . In this you will have repented. It is said, "If you want to repent, practice zazen and understand reality." That is repentance. If you feel you've wronged someone, you should sit earnestly. In that way you will build [a foundation for] yourself.

Little by little, you will advance until you reach the end. Your karma will be erased and you will doubtlessly improve physically. Whatever happens, there will be nothing to worry about.[8]

Zazen is not something reserved for when you sit. Humans already live in Tathagata (*Nyōrai*) Zen. This [Tathagata Zen] already *is*. It's the original enlightenment of the whole universe; it is "thus" (*nyō*). And the place deep inside of us is "comes" (*rai*). We sit in this "thus come" (*nyōrai*). What we call "I" is the whole universe. It is here where we must sit. All we need to do is stop [creating] delusion. Just stop the three poisons, which means stop and sit.

As long as we are alive we are creating delusion because we are fumbling through life. We call this living. We have to quit this way of living.

"Then," you say, "I might as well hang myself." That's not right. We have to quit within this life of fumbling. We have to practice within it. No matter what circumstances manifest, we have to act within them. That is the meaning of living in the "truth of all dharmas." There you actually sit in no-mind. Practicing this activity of non-ego, you will without a doubt make contact with the true wisdom. You can't make contact through your mind. But you will clearly realize it as the way to peace. You will feel truly grateful.

All of you please treat this "sitting mind" with great care in your life.[9]

O

I remember having dinner with Ikebe and Shūko in their small, rickety old country house. It was immaculately kept; even the wobbly non-flush toilet was spotless. Ikebe's demeanor, too, was that of a woman who paid scrupulous attention to detail. Though she was old and frail by the time I knew her, the careful attention she paid to every aspect of her life was quite impressive. There was an elegant simplicity about her that reminded me of Yokoyama in his little haunt in the park.

---

[8] From the last of the *Dō Tankyū no Shisei* series, *Nyōze*, July 27, 1994.
[9] From "*Iki ni Kiku*" (*Listening to the Breath*), *Nyōze*, May 27, 1995.

Both teachers were raised in upper-class families in the early 1900s, but it was impossible to tell how much of their elegant deportment was a result of a strict upbringing in a society that greatly valued proper behavior and how much came from an awareness cultivated through their Zen practice.

What stood out to me with regard to Ikebe was how similar her attitude was to the evolving American ideals of what we might call a Gaian or ecological Buddhism—a Buddhism in which we see ourselves as sisters and brothers of the living Earth. Though Ikebe gave humans, with their ability to reflect, a special place among God's creature, she also asserted (like the Buddhist ecologists) that "human beings, birds, animals, insects, trees and grasses, and all things down to the tiniest pebbles are all equal." Above all, Ikebe exemplified this belief in her life, which was a testament to her concern for all beings, sentient and non-sentient.

5 DYING IN ZAZEN

KŌSHŌ UCHIYAMA

I never took either lay or monk's ordination under Kōshō Uchiyama, yet I thought of him as my teacher during my stay in Japan. Though I knew him more intimately than any of the others, I never felt a special desire to tell his story. Kōdō Sawaki, a scholar and teacher orphaned to a crooked gambler and his eleventh wife; Sodō Yokoyama, sitting in a park practicing zazen, brushing poetry and playing the grass flute; Kōzan Katō, telling his story at ninety-four years old, a story of zazen and of wandering the country in poverty; and Motoko Ikebe, female artist, astrologer, and Zen teacher, moving into the country to live off the land; these were all colorful figures whose stories begged to be told. But it was Uchiyama's zazen teaching that I learned, and it was his zazen schedule that I followed, and it was Uchiyama whom I went to when I felt confused about what I was doing in Japan.

I clearly was not taken by Uchiyama's charismatic personality, because I didn't feel he had one; and since I mistakenly equated charisma with wisdom, I also often missed Uchiyama's Buddhism. I had come to Japan in order to find the exotic, and met a teacher whose rational thinking struck me as nothing out of the ordinary.

After my first sesshin at Antaiji, as we were sitting around drinking tea, Uchiyama asked me if I felt as though something were missing (*monotarinai*). This was a question I would hear him ask many people in subsequent sesshins. He assumed this feeling of something missing would be a part of all of our zazen experiences and the important teaching was learning to accept it. Sitting was not some kind of excitement to him. It was sitting with boredom, pain, fatigue, dissatisfaction, or whatever came up. Enlightened living for him was living with the mundane.

"Just sit," he would say, "and watch thoughts go by. Treat them as the scenery in your life." And, "If you sit at Antaiji for ten years, eating brown rice and vegetables, with few toys, you will learn to rely on yourself, to sit through boredom and accept it." That was his explanation of the religious life.

So, with all my confusion about Uchiyama the man—why he didn't act as I imagined Zen masters to act—there was a teaching of zazen that to this day I hold in the highest regard, a zazen that doesn't look for special feelings or states, a zazen that teaches you to sit through it all, the ups and downs, the fears and anxieties and joys.

Uchiyama was what the Japanese call a *"botchan,"* a pampered child, raised without being required to take care of his own personal needs. This is common in Japan, especially in privileged families. To varying degrees, most of the members of the international community who came to Antaiji were similarly pampered. With his background, Uchiyama was better prepared to understand us than his predecessor Sawaki, who had lived a hard life, would have been.

Our suffering, like his, was primarily psychological rather than physical. If we were temporarily "poor," it was usually by choice; we were living in a country with little poverty and plenty of opportunity to make money.

Of course our "suffering," if I may be allowed to call it that, was not unlike that of the Buddha's. According to legend, the Buddha suffered from the fact that pain, old age, and death were unavoidable. But he, too, being young and healthy when he left home to seek enlightenment, was not actually experiencing any of those sufferings.

Uchiyama boasted of not having worked more than six months in his entire life. This was certainly not the kind of thing a Japanese person would usually speak proudly of, but it would not have surprised me to hear a similar claim from any of the Antaiji international community. Throughout most of my stay in Japan, for example, I worked only on Wednesdays, and my wife remembers with amusement how upset I was every Tuesday night at the thought of the next day's work.

Uchiyama's attitude was very similar to that of many of the Kyoto international community at that time: we didn't want to be controlled by what we felt was a society driven by economic forces. For many priests in Japan, Buddhism was nothing more than a family business, important, perhaps, to their community, but having little connection with true religious principles. The institutional Buddhism flourishing in Japan had few abbots who saw the inherent contradiction in the economically driven Buddhist priest, but it was clear to Uchiyama.

Though Uchiyama might have seemed a bit prudish to those growing up in the promiscuous sixties in the United States, he was quite modern compared to his peers in Japan. For one thing, he had an unusual background for the abbot of a Zen temple, having been married twice before becoming a monk. Both wives died shortly afterward, one as a result of tuberculosis and the second in childbirth. Uchiyama describes himself as quite confused during this period in his life, and even blames himself for the early death of his wives. "I killed them with my selfishness," he said, reflecting years later on his tumultuous life before shaving his head. His third marriage, which occurred twenty-five years after becoming a monk, he describes in much more sober terms than his first two. His first two were marriages of love and confusion, the last one was of consideration and practicality, though anyone who saw him in retirement with Keiko was aware of their mutual affection.

Uchiyama saw a great deal of value in the cultural encounters between his Japanese disciples and his Western students. At times, however, he found himself walking a tightrope when dealing with the differing social mores of the two groups, particularly when it came to sexual matters.

Robert, a nineteen-year-old American, came to Antaiji about a year and a half after I arrived. His desire to be a member of the club was transparent. I remember walking around Gentaku one day with him in his newly acquired monk's work clothes, head shaven, and listening to his first sermon. He talked to me about love. "I experienced true love once," he said, "and now I'm done with it." "Indeed!" I thought to myself. Our talk ended with Robert recommending I read *The Art of Loving* by Eric Fromm.

After some months at Antaiji, Robert had demonstrated that he could take part in the schedule at the temple with the energy and enthusiasm of a novice monk and was granted his wish to be ordained by Uchiyama. He received a new name, Jōei. Jōei looked handsome in his new robes and attracted the attention of a new woman named Von, who had come to Antaiji from Canada to practice zazen. It wasn't long before the two were a couple. Jōei was passionately in love for a second time. Feeling he couldn't continue seeing Von while living at Antaiji, he took up residence with her at a nearby apartment. He wanted to continue sitting at Antaiji and asked Uchiyama for permission to do so.

"Are you and Von living together?" Uchiyama asked.

Jōei replied in the affirmative.

"In that case you'd better not come to sit with us." And that was the end of Jōei's relationship to Antaiji.

I'm sure Uchiyama was disappointed that his first Western disciple left the temple soon after being ordained, but there was more to his decision than disappointment. Monks at Antaiji were expected to be refraining from sexual relationships while they were training. Those who went on to run their own temples after they completed their training usually married, but while living and training at Antaiji they understood sexual relationships were not permitted. I don't know whether other monks had sexual relations while living at Antaiji, but if any did, it was in secret. Uchiyama had to think about what kind of message he would have been sending the other monks if he permitted a newly ordained disciple to have a girlfriend while training at Antaiji. Uchiyama did not seem to believe that monks needed to avoid relationships with women altogether, but he did feel it necessary for them to refrain from sexual relationships while training at Antaiji.

I dropped by the temple after lunch once after I had moved out of Antaiji and was living nearby. At Antaiji you could walk in and talk with monks without an invitation, as long as there was no special program on at the time. You usually made an appointment to see Uchiyama if you had something to discuss with him, but that wasn't absolutely necessary. If he was free, he was willing to see you on a moment's notice.

I was troubled by my powerful desire for sex. Because I had come to Japan to learn Zen meditation and hoped to devote at least a year exclusively to that, this growing sexual tension seem obsessive and obstructive—but there it was, and I wanted to ask Uchiyama for some advice. At the same time, I felt embarrassed bothering him with a question about my personal appetites. The monks and Uchiyama were sitting on the veranda making small talk. He welcomed me into the circle. Knowing I didn't usually drop by at that time, he turned to me and asked:

"Did you have something special you wanted to talk about?"

"Yes," I said meekly.

"Can we talk here?" he asked.

I didn't want to talk in front of all the monks about my personal sexual issues. On the other hand, I felt that requiring a private meeting to discuss such mundane problems was self-indulgent. I was in conflict. I sheepishly said it would be okay to talk there.

"What is it?" he asked. I could see the monks perking up as something outside the realm of normal lunch conversation was about to be discussed.

Hesitating, I said, "It's about me and women."

The monks were delighted. This was even better than they had hoped for.

Uchiyama's countenance changed and he said, "Come into my room."

The expressions on the faces of most of the monks dropped as we walked down the hallway and into his room.

"Now what's the problem?" he continued.

"I'm not exactly sure," I said. "I know that I came eight thousand miles to study and practice Buddhism and hoped to put my worldly desires on hold during this time. But I find myself needing female companionship more now than ever. Immediately after sesshin, I usually end up in a coffee shop, hoping to find a girlfriend."

He looked at me and, without much deliberation, said, "You're not the only one, you know. I, too, have been through this a number of times. I married my present wife after Sawaki Roshi died, but it wasn't the first time I'd fallen in love. Your situation is quite normal. Just watch these feelings while you sit. If you can't see them as the scenery in your life, that is, if you are constantly bothered, then you may have to get off your cushion and do something about it."

This response to my ticklish confession put me at ease. We talked a bit more about love and Japanese and American differences in dealing with it, and I left feeling relaxed and better about myself. I also said goodbye to a group of very disappointed monks.

Of the five teachers in this book, Sawaki and his disciple Yokoyama never married. Many of Sawaki's disciples considered it a sign of weak resolve for a priest to get married. Uchiyama, Sawaki's closest disciple, knew his decision to marry would not go over very well with many of his teacher's disciples, and his explanations for marrying seemed at times contrived. At one talk he said he married "to keep the young women from hanging all over him"—a remark that earned chuckles from his audience.

But Uchiyama's more serious justification for marrying was that he didn't want his disciples to have to take care of him in old age, as had happened with Sawaki. He often referred to the period of nursing Sawaki during the master's final years as the most intense religious practice in his life. Though he wasn't the only one responsible for Sawaki's care—Jōshin, Antaiji's nun also participated—he was in charge of the group that did so.

Once when Uchiyama referred in a lecture to the work he did caring for Sawaki as "a crowning teaching," my wife Hiroko turned to me and said, "That's a crowning teaching? Most Japanese women take that for granted as part of their life's duty." In that lecture Uchiyama talked specifically about having to wipe Sawaki's buttocks. "They were so sore," he said, "that I wiped them with my hand, not wanting to irritate his skin any further." In addition to the normal burden of caring for an elderly, ill, bedridden patient, Uchiyama faced the additional challenge of tending a man who had fended for himself and relished his independence for eighty-three years.

SAWAKI'S FINAL YEARS

Sawaki was a man who kept on the move. Even in his old age, his untiring devotion to practice as he lectured on the Way and ran zazen retreats around the country was unprecedented. He shuttled between Komazawa University in Tokyo, Antaiji in Kyoto, and other temples and training dōjōs in Nagoya, Kyūshū, and Tōhoku in northern Honshū. He traveled by public transportation without an attendant even into his eighties and valued his independence. At age eighty-three, from early February he went to Myōgenji in Nagoya, and from there to Hiroshima, Yamaguchi, Saga, Kurume, Oita, and Matsuyama, returning to Kyoto in mid-March. At that time his health began to fail seriously and he started feeling the cold more and suffered from fatigue, but it was only when he could no longer walk that he gave up this life as a wandering teacher and settled in one place.

When Uchiyama received a telegram that Sawaki sent from Tokyo reading, "Please come and pick me up," Uchiyama went immediately and brought his teacher back to Antaiji. From that time until his death two and one-half years later, Uchiyama was Sawaki's attendant and nurse. Sawaki was lodged in the only second-floor room in the temple, with a large deciduous tree that kept the summer sun from getting too hot, and once its leaves had fallen allowed the winter sun in, making for year-round comfort. Here Sawaki read, met students, and lectured.

Perhaps as a result of being forced to slow down and live in a room that provided protection against extremes of temperature and the rigors of travel, Sawaki started to feel better. He never again had the free use of his legs, but he returned to his lively self. "There's nothing wrong with me," he was quoted as saying, "except the fact that I can't walk."

He could hardly leave the temple. As the warm weather came, he was able to take short walks around the Antaiji grounds with Uchiyama's assistance, but his legs grew worse again and even these short walks came to an end.

Uchiyama started taking his teacher to an acupuncturist in Kyoto, but there was no change in the condition of his legs. He then concentrated on Sawaki's diet, feeding him nutritious foods with the hope that healing his entire system would improve the condition of his legs. Sawaki's health did improve as a result of his new diet and the forced rest, and those who came to hear his talks and to receive instructions from him sensed a renewed energy. But in spite of a laundry list of treatments, each recommended by one of the many visitors who came pouring in—shiatsu, acupuncture, moxibustion, Chinese herbal medicine, *seitai* (a variety of Japanese chiropractic manipulation), soaking his feet in a mugwort potion, enzymatic baths, static electricity therapy— the condition of Sawaki's legs remained unchanged.

When Sawaki first came to settle at Antaiji in June 1963 he was walking in the garden, but by the spring of 1965 he could only leave his second-floor room about once every ten days. He spent his last days confined to reading in his room.

As early as the fall of 1963 he was already talking about his end. Tadao Tanaka, his biographer, visited him and quoted him as saying, "I know death must be coming soon, though I don't feel its presence one bit." Long before he was forced to settle at Antaiji, he had his last will and testament hanging on his person. It stated: "If this rustic monk is found dead by the roadside, take his body to a nearby university to be dissected and used for research." He always carried 5000 yen, which he requested be used for transporting his corpse, with a tip for the trouble he'd caused.

As it became more difficult for Sawaki to leave his room, Uchiyama spent extra time with him on the second floor. In the morning Antaiji residents and guests who had spent the night would join Sawaki for tea and quiet conversation. At about 9:30 AM Uchiyama would go to him with a pot of green tea and they would talk of events of the day and of things Uchiyama had read in the newspaper. Sawaki hadn't read the newspaper much in his wandering days, but now Uchiyama brought him magazines and discussed the major events in the news in an attempt to keep his teacher from dying of boredom as a result of this unfamiliar confinement. "His eyes had gotten so bad," Tanaka wrote, "that he had to resort to a magnifying glass or binoculars in order to read."

Tanaka quoted Sawaki as saying in 1965: "It's difficult for me to go up and down the stairs so they have to carry the wash basin up to me here. Uchiyama, Jōshin, and others bathe me. I'm like a newborn baby." Sawaki would try to make them laugh while they bathed him. When they finished and he was relaxing, feeling better, he would say, "I'm so lucky" and "This is too good for me."

Tanaka writes: "There were ten of us in the room one day that summer and Roshi talked for twenty minutes about the lines 'How many miles from the floating world / Mountain cherry' from a well-known Japanese poem. But his voice was not as in the old days, and it was not unusual to see his whole body or his hands shaking. I thought of the great monks of old, and I felt his deterioration and was filled with emotion. Tears started to roll down my face and I went to the toilet and cried my eyes out."

In the monthly magazine *Henshō* (Reflection) Uchiyama recorded Sawaki's final days. He described a Buddhist lecture Sawaki gave to some nuns in June 1965: "Roshi was feeling good. He knew this would be his last lecture to these nuns so he stretched himself to his limits. When he finished he was exhausted. However, after the lecture, he was asked to brush paintings on a bunch of fans for people from Jumanji Temple." Uchiyama goes on to say that at the end of World War II, when there was little food to spare in Japan, Uchiyama and a number of other of Sawaki's disciples were sheltered and fed at Jumanji. Sawaki never had a chance to repay the temple for taking care of his disciples, so he couldn't refuse this favor despite the fact that he was worn out from the lecture.

From Sawaki's window you could see Takagamine, one of the three peaks in the northwest of Kyoto. This was the peak where Tosui, an Edo-period Zen eccentric, spent his final days. Tosui, like Jittoku, Kanzan, and Hotei, was a character Sawaki often referred to with great respect. One of the final joys of Sawaki's life was looking out at Takagamine and watching the clouds quietly pass over the peak. Tosui composed a poem in which he spent his final days gazing at Takagamine Peak. I'm sure Sawaki's joy at looking out at the peak was partly from knowing that one of his favorite eccentrics shared the same pleasure more than two hundred years earlier.

There were others besides Uchiyama and Jōshin who came to help care for Sawaki. One, a nun by the name of Kōbun Okamoto, was the abbess of Myōgenji, a nunnery in Nagoya. Kōbun reported that when she went to Sawaki's room and started to straighten up around him, he pointed to the window and beckoned her, "Come here and look at Takagamine. Lately, that mountain has been calling me. It's saying, 'Kōdō,' Kōdō.'" Kōbun said that she couldn't find any words to respond because she was so choked with emotion.

With Sawaki's failing health and continued confinement to bed, he turned his attention more and more to the mountain, Takagamine. He could gaze out at it through the southern window while lying there. It was lying there beside him. He had spent much of his life in the mountains throughout Japan, living in them and walking through them, and watching his beloved Takagamine proved to be an important consolation in his final days.

Sawaki had been in a coma for some days when he stopped breathing at 1:50 AM on December 21. In accord with his wishes, he was taken to the dissection room of the Kyoto University Medical School. Word of Sawaki's death spread and many friends and disciples who lived nearby came to the dissection room to get a last look at Roshi's face.

Tanaka writes of leaving the medical school and returning to Antaiji. In the entrance was a picture of Sawaki behind a stream of smoke from incense sticks. Alongside the picture was a statement of appreciation to those who came to pay their last respects to him, with an explanation of Sawaki's wish to have his body used for medical research, and a note stating that Roshi didn't want any funeral or farewell service of any kind. It was also written that all those who came to pay their last respects to Roshi should come into the temple and do zazen, however long or short. Roshi derived joy from a life of zazen, it went on to say, and that zazen was for him the deepest of treasures.

After a period of zazen, Tanaka turned to Uchiyama, bowed to him, and thanked him for taking care of Sawaki for the last two and one-half years.

"There isn't going to be a funeral, is there?" Tanaka asked.

"If I had to perform a formal funeral according to Sōtō-sect rules, I would sneak away at night. I know nothing about complicated ceremonies," was Uchiyama's response.

All of Roshi's students at Antaiji got together and decided to hold a forty-nine-day sesshin immediately. Forty-nine days, the "in-between state" or *bardo*, popularized in Tibetan Buddhism, actually has its roots in Theravada and Mahayana works of the second century. It is considered the time between death and the following rebirth of an individual. There is a Japanese Buddhist service after forty-nine days celebrating the moment that the individual has chosen a new birth. The Antaiji group decided to take this ritual and turn it into something that would have meaning in light of Sawaki's teaching, hence the forty-nine-day sesshin.

Friends and disciples of Sawaki from all over the country came to Antaiji to take part in this farewell sesshin. In Tanaka's words it was a "sublime Buddhist service for a man who devoted his life to zazen."

Sawaki was a symbol of the ancient Zen man for many people throughout Japan. His straight talk and simple lifestyle touched the imaginations of those who longed for a Buddhism they believed was a part of the "good old days." Sawaki was also an entertaining speaker with a wealth of knowledge of the scriptures. His energy and his mobility brought the practice of zazen to many remote parts of Japan.

OLD BUDDHA KATŌ

If Sawaki was the emissary for zazen, his friend Kōzan Katō was the embodiment of the practice. While Sawaki toured Japan preaching zazen and, in his articulate way, describing the practice for all to understand, his less articulate friend Katō just sat. When Katō did talk, he might mumble something barely comprehensible about the importance of zazen, but his very presence was so joyful that he was more convincing than the most polished orator. His simple life and strong commitment to zazen won him the respect of Sawaki.

Katō, four years Sawaki's senior, thought to visit his friend when he heard Sawaki's health was failing. Sawaki was reported to have said there was no reason for the "old man" to plod all the way to Kyoto to visit him—a remark made out of a wish not to inconvenience his friend and also, perhaps, to assert his independence. Katō took Sawaki on his word and didn't go to Kyoto. On his deathbed, however, Sawaki expressed his desire to see his old friend. Unfortunately, that wish was only reported to Katō after Sawaki's death, so the meeting never took place.

Katō was approaching ninety at the time and had a wife and family, and a trip to Antaiji for the "farewell sesshin" may have been beyond his capacity. Still his absence at the celebration of zazen must have been conspicuous.

> *The wind is fresh*
> *The moon bright*
> *Let us spend the evening dancing*
> *As a farewell to old age.*

Though written over one hundred fifty years before Kōzan Katō's death, this poem by Ryōkan would have been a fitting tribute to a man whose true influence as a Buddhist teacher emerged in his nineties.

Though I had read Katō's life in his own words as well as accounts of his teaching reported by one of his two dharma heirs, there was still so much about which I was uncertain. Though Katō's two Dharma heirs were dead, there was still his temple, Tokuunin, run by his son Taigan. I knew I had to go there and see what I could learn.

In 1985 I started to translate *Living in Zazen* after carrying the book around for ten years. I went to visit Yūzen Yanase, Katō's only remaining Dharma heir. I met him at his temple and spent the night talking about his teacher and left with his permission to translate *Living in Zazen*. I gave up the project after a few chapters, feeling that the sense I was getting from reading the book in its original was not translating well into English. But I continued to reread the book, enjoying it more each time. Yanase Roshi had mentioned to me that Katō's son was in charge of Tokuunin, but it took me fifteen years to decide to search out Tokuunin. Yanase had died over ten years earlier. If I didn't act quickly, I thought, there would be no one left to talk to who had any memories of Katō.

Tokuunin is a small temple in a little town outside of Tokyo. I didn't have an address and there were only a couple of days remaining on my Japan Railroad pass, after which my travel would be confined to the Osaka-Kyoto area for lack of funds, so I started doing some detective work. I found out that Tokuunin was a branch temple of Kenchōji monastery, a large head temple in Kamakura, and I was certain I could find out more about Tokuunin there.[1]

I hadn't been to Kamakura in thirty years and I was very excited to return, but that excitement began to wane quickly from the moment I got off the train. It was

---

[1] Zen head temples serve as administrative and spiritual centers for the organizations that oversee the branch temples. There are fifteen head temples in Rinzai Zen, and Kenchōji is the second largest. It has 406 branch temples under its administration, of which Tokuunin is one.

the height of summer, and Kamakura was particularly hot and humid that day, filled with crowds visiting this city of temples and of the Great Buddha. I took a bus to the stop nearest the temple and slipped into a snake of people eight to ten wide. While the line inched forward, I was carried past the temple (there were other famous temples in the vicinity), and reversing my direction wasn't easy. I finally made my way into the line for Kenchōji and worked my way to the entrance gate where tickets to enter the temple grounds were sold.

I asked the people at the ticket gate to let me in to inquire about Tokuunin. They directed me to the administration office. I got lost in the maze of Kenchōji's numerous buildings, but finally found the administration office—only to be ignored by the monks there whom I hoped might help me. Ordinary Japanese people are generally quite friendly and helpful, but "important" Japanese, especially those who don't speak English (still the majority), can be masters at pretending you are not there. The longer I associate with the Japanese, the more intimidating I find this behavior—a sign that the culture is rubbing off on me, for this is how ordinary Japanese feel in the same situation.

I ran back to the Kenchōji ticket gate and the people working there helpfully found a directory of branch temples in the Kenchōji line, gave me the address and phone number of Tokuunin, complimented me on my Japanese, and all in all gave me a brighter outlook on the human race.

I called Taigan at Tokuunin from a kiosk outside of Kenchōji, not without some trepidation. I hoped that he had inherited the kindness and warmth that impressed me so much about his father in *Living in Zazen*, but still, calling the head priest of a temple out of the blue, with no introduction, made me somewhat anxious. Taigan immediately put me at ease when he began to speak over the telephone. There was no Zen posturing, just the voice of a friendly, middle-aged Japanese man trying to accommodate my request. I explained that I was writing about his father and wanted to see the temple and talk with him. He asked me if a few days hence would be acceptable, and when he saw my hesitation, asked what my schedule was. I explained that I was in Kamakura on my way to Tokyo, and that I had two more days on my JR railroad pass, after which I should be getting back to Kyoto. He explained that he was meeting a Polish couple the next day around eleven in the morning but, considering my situation, it would be OK for me to join them. Though I felt I might be intruding, I jumped at the invitation.

After spending the night at a friend's house in Tokyo, I left early in the morning to arrive at my appointment on time. Having grown up using the New York subways, I allowed plenty of time for delays. This, coupled with my anticipation, resulted in my arriving two hours early. Though I knew I was violating Japanese etiquette by arriving early, I also wanted to have as much time alone with Taigan as possible, so I called and said that I had arrived at the station quite early. He kindly told me I was welcome to come right over. The directions from the train station were a bit confusing to me, so I took a cab.

In ten minutes I found myself looking down on the temple from a road that must have been carved out of the mountain with the temple at its foot. The modest compound of two small buildings with a river running along the far side of the valley was no longer the dilapidated old temple described in *Living in Zazen*. There were plum trees everywhere and I was reminded of Katō saying he started planting plum trees as soon as he arrived at Tokuunin. He'd been dead twenty-eight years already and his plum trees were still there—still standing, though showing the inevitable signs of their age. Taigan later told me that the trees his father planted no longer produced edible fruit, but he had planted new ones next to them; the old trees stood there like elders guiding their young offspring, just as the words of Katō guided his son.

I stood there for a moment, enjoying the excitement of seeing this temple that had played a part in my imaginings for over twenty years. Knowing that he walked along that road, that he planted those trees, was enough to lift me out of my mundane thoughts and make my steps a little bit lighter. The fact that the buildings were no longer in disrepair cast a pall over my romantic vision of Katō's world, but then there were unexpected, pleasant surprises: a dog, two cats and a goat. The temple was still a country temple, and the spirit of Katō, the "farmer-monk" as he referred to himself, was still very much alive.

Taigan's wife greeted me at the entrance and led me to the smaller building that housed the Zen meditation hall and the meeting room. I waited there looking around at the few decorations, a photo of the temple and Katō's calligraphy. Taigan appeared, we bowed to each other, and quickly arrived at my reason for coming: to hear about Katō from his son's perspective. I told him that I was writing about his father and that all of my information came from the book *Living in Zazen* and its reprint with the appendix "Kōzan Katō's *Zuimonki*."

"Just one minute," he said, and left the room and came back with two small books and a magazine. His wife brought in the tea and a sweet.

"Sendai" ("the previous abbot," the name he used to refer to his father) "said we shouldn't record any of his talks. Just listen and then drop it. I struggled with that for a long time. Finally I decided to go ahead and publish these books, but I haven't put them on the market. I just give them to people who come here with an interest in Sendai's teaching."

I was quite excited to have this new material.

Taigan's wife sat with us, and it became apparent to me that she too derived pleasure from talking about her father-in-law. She joined in our talk and was as animated as her husband when they talked about Sendai and the good old days.

"Did you know Roshi before you married Taigan-san?" I asked her.

"Yes my father studied with him for many years."

We had some more tea and there was an uncomfortable silence as we looked down at our teacups. I realized that they wanted to know what I was interested in and were waiting for me to talk.

"Roshi's other children didn't follow in his footsteps did they?" I asked rhetorically.

"Sendai recommended zazen to everyone except his children. He never had us read sutras either. 'It's better to know nothing,' he would say. He felt that if we wanted to practice we would, but felt it was better not to push us. I know that he was happy when I decided to become a monk."

"Where did you train?" I asked.

"I trained at Kenchōji. Tokuunin is a branch temple of Kenchōji. The Roshi there had studied with Sendai. He couldn't believe I didn't know any of the sutras. I didn't even know the correct way to sit zazen. I was the only monk there who had no background in the practice. Nobody could believe it," he said laughing.

"I'd read in the afterword of *Living in Zazen* that Roshi died in the seated position," which I took to be Akizuki's way of saying he died in the lotus position. "Was that just a romantic notion of Professor Akizuki's?"

"Sendai's last day?" he said half to himself.

"A businessman, a Mr. Yui, who had built a house nearby Tokuunin in order to have regular dharma interviews with Sendai came that morning. At eleven-thirty he met with another disciple, Minoru Satō." I later learned that this Minoru Satō was Taigan's wife's father. "They talked about zazen. Sendai quoted, 'Zazen is the supreme Way of Heaven and Earth.' After saying this, he turned to Mr. Satō and said, 'I am carrying on this Way. Practicing in this manner is what I call satori.' He then inscribed a *tōba*, a wooden tablet, for the seventh day after the death of a parishioner. He turned the tōba around, inscribed the date on it, and turned it around once more. After the inscription he wrote the character *katsu*, a Zen shout.

"Mr. Satō went home and told his wife about Sendai inscribing the tōba and they were both thrilled that he was apparently healthy again. He had been weak for the last month and everyone was worried about him. My mother went to the kitchen to prepare a sandwich for his lunch and when she returned he was lying down. He had fallen over. He never regained consciousness and died that evening."

Taigan showed me the zendō. Along the center of the far wall was the traditional Zen altar with the statue of Shakyamuni Buddha in the center. Near the left corner of the same wall was a small wooden statue of Katō, a thin man with a large protruding belly (his trademark). Near the right corner of the wall was a small statue of Sawaki. The family never forgot their father's debt to Sawaki, who helped Katō survive the war years. Sawaki's regular visits to Tokuunin every New Year's holiday brought him closer and closer to the family. It was a moving experience to see a zendō with these two Zen men with such different approaches to zazen joined together on both sides of Shakyamuni, the main image of the hall.

We then walked outside and stood by the river.

"Do you follow your father's schedule?" I asked.

"I get up at four every morning and do zazen. Then I recite the *Risshūbun* (the sutra Katō recited), but not as loud as Sendai," he said laughing.

"I was happy to see the goat. I never expected to see one in a modern temple."

"We always gave Sendai goat's milk. It helped him stay healthy."

This conversation, followed by a talk about the plum trees (which Taigan continues to plant), made me realize what a large figure Katō was in his son's life. He lived under the shadow of his father, but it was not an intimidating shadow—it was more like living in the shade of a willow tree. As these thoughts were going through my head, Taigan's wife came to tell us that the other two guests had arrived.

The Polish couple were artists and Zen practitioners who had heard about Kōzan Katō and wanted to learn more. They were very enthusiastic about Zen and Japan and knew the proper protocol: they had brought a cake that the husband baked for the occasion; they had come after writing a formal letter and making an appointment in advance; when they were given cushions to sit on, they refused, saying they preferred the tatami floor in the summer. In spite of my many years in Japan, I was quickly developing an inferiority complex: my present was sweets purchased at the station near the temple; I'd called without an introduction and pushed my way in that day; after two hours seated in formal Japanese style, my knees were hurting so bad I wanted to put the two cushions offered to them on top of mine.

After lunch Taigan took the three of us to the train station and we said our goodbyes. As I watched him drive away I realized that I still had many questions. Some would never be answered, perhaps.

IN SEARCH OF SODŌ YOKOYAMA'S DISCIPLE

I was a little anxious about looking up Yokoyama's sole disciple Jōkō Shibata, too. I had met him once almost twenty-five years earlier at Antaiji, and I was sure he wouldn't remember me.

But when I called him and told him that I got his phone number from Uchiyama's wife, Keiko, he invited me to come and visit him. His voice on the phone, like Taigan's, was warm and informal and my nervousness quickly dissolved.

The first time I'd ever seen Jōkō Shibata was in 1971, when he accompanied his teacher Sodō Yokoyama to the yearly memorial celebration for Kōdō Sawaki at Antaiji. Jōkō had been training at Antaiji prior to this, but had left the temple after observing Yokoyama sitting in zazen there. He decided on the spot to apprentice himself to Yokoyama: "I saw my teacher in zazen and I knew then that I would study with him."

He approached Yokoyama to be accepted as his disciple, but the master refused and asked him to continue practicing at Antaiji. Yokoyama told Jōkō that his lifestyle could not accommodate a disciple since he had no temple and a very small income, but Jōkō was not easily dissuaded. He left Antaiji, went to Komoro where Yokoyama lived and pleaded to be accepted until the master finally acquiesced. Yokoyama asked his new disciple to train for a few years at Eiheiji before coming to live with him. I've often wondered whether the master was buying time so that he could figure out what to do with this new and unexpected situation.

I had come to Jōkō in order to find out about the final years of his teacher. While he spoke about his teacher and about Sawaki, his teacher's teacher, I was receiving an unexpected bonus. Jōkō was as completely devoted to the practice of zazen as his teachers, if not more so. He may not have possessed the dynamism and charisma of Sawaki or the elegance and artistic sensibility of Yokoyama, but his faith in zazen was great enough to make him a fitting heir to carry on the work of his two predecessors. And it was, after all, an interest in zazen that encouraged me to learn more about these teachers.

Jōkō was in his mid-fifties at the time of our meeting. He welcomed me into his home, peering through horn-rimmed glasses with a smile on his face. His reserve quickly dropped away as we got to know each other.

My timing was perfect. Jōkō had just quit his job at a *miso* factory (he had always worked for a living, even while living with Yokoyama) and completed the construction of a new zendō. Now after more than twenty years he had enough money saved to retire—provided he lived a very frugal life. That he did.

He led me through the hallway to a modest-sized zendō perhaps as large as the rest of the house, where I placed my gift in front of a small picture of his teacher seated in zazen. On the other side of the altar was a picture of Kōdō Sawaki, also in zazen. I lit incense at the altar, we bowed, and then we returned to the small parlor at the entrance to the zendō. Jōkō boiled water for tea. It was a gloomy twilight evening.

I didn't really know Jōkō, his interests, his lifestyle, or his feeling about my visit. I told him of the reason for coming to see him: to find out about Yokoyama's final days. Why, I asked, did he die at seventy-four? Though not young, he seemed so healthy when I met him, much healthier than Uchiyama, his younger brother disciple, who was still going strong into his eighties at the time of this meeting. It was a rather silly question, really, but it was a way to open the conversation and Jōkō accepted it. In fact, he responded in a way I never imagined, leaving me with my mouth open and jaw hanging.

"I feel somewhat responsible for his early death," he said, "I should have taken more care to feed him better."

My only knowledge of Jōkō's cooking came from the article by Kyūji Inoue about his visit to Kaikoen, in which he wrote, "purple mushrooms, gingko nuts, chrysanthemum petals—rare treats . . . so delicious that even I, whose appetite has declined of late, found myself overeating." I reminded Jōkō of Inoue's description of his cooking, but he laughed it off.

"Of course he would say that. Wouldn't you if you were a guest at someone's house? You're obligated to say that, aren't you? I have my regrets. If only I were a bit more skilled at cooking and a little more knowledgeable about nutrition. . . . I truly feel that."

As he continued, I realized that I wasn't going to convince him that he wasn't responsible for his teachers early death so I just listened passively.

"My teacher used to go to the park during the coldest part of winter. Little by little he exhausted all his energy. He lived with the bare minimum—in poverty. In fact, he perfected this life of poverty."

Jōkō was certainly following his teacher's way in this respect. The only possible extravagance apparent to me in his life was the new zendō, of which he said: "This was something my teacher had hoped to do, but it was never possible for him. So I am doing it in his stead."

Here was a zendō that could sit fifteen or twenty people, virtually unused. Jōkō, who sat most of the day, sat on the veranda to get the cool breeze in summer and the sun in winter. I was sure, whether he admitted it to himself or not, that he was not comfortable in the new zendō. I came there to find out about Yokoyama's final years, but my interest in this monk, Yokoyama's lone disciple, was distracting me—though it was certainly a very pleasant and even valuable distraction. Yokoyama had simplified his life as the monks of old did. He went to the park, played the grass flute, brushed poems, and sat zazen. He interrupted this schedule only three days a year when he visited Antaiji for his teacher's memorial ceremony. Jōkō had carried this ascetic lifestyle even further.

Jōkō didn't compose poems, practice calligraphy, or play the leaf. He listened to his teacher and his teacher's teacher talk about zazen. For both his predecessors, zazen was "the most important practice for humankind." Jōkō read the books of Sawaki's lectures and the works of Dōgen, and he practiced zazen from eight to ten hours a day. "That's about all I can do," he said. "I get tired when I do more than ten hours." He wasn't talking about sesshin; this was his daily routine.

I forgot about Yokoyama for a moment and asked Jōkō about zazen.

"Thoughts naturally arise," he began, "but you shouldn't follow them. When you are thinking, you will slump. When I sit across from a mirror, I can really see this. When I am wrapped up in thought and I glance at a mirror, I see how my posture is. Sure enough, something is off.

"Human beings are thinkers. We can't rid ourselves of thinking. But we don't have to chase after thoughts or wipe them away. Of course what I am suggesting is not easy.

"When we think we tend to chase after thoughts. So when we are doing that we just have to correct our posture. Thinking is not good, but chasing after thoughts or trying to erase them is no good either. This is why posture is so important. You think and your posture crumbles. You correct it. You think again and your neck or your torso bends, or some other part of your body slips, and again you correct it. Keep your posture right, leaving things as they are.

"There is good-feeling zazen too," he continued. "'Ah this feels great.' In fact, this too is not really good zazen. When you are feeling, 'this is good zazen,' just check yourself and you will see. You may think 'this is wonderful, the time flew by while I was sitting.' But if you check your posture during these times, you'll see your mind is actually wandering.

"You really have to give all your effort to it. It's not easy to do this kind of zazen. Still you have to keep aiming for it. When you do that and your body is in the correct position, you will feel it. Then the feeling 'this is fine' will become apparent. It will happen naturally. 'Ah, I should just sit—this is the way of the universe.'"

With the word universe I was brought back to Yokoyama, the man I had come there to learn more about, but I didn't stop Jōkō as he enthusiastically talked about his favorite subject. I told myself that I was hearing a distillation of his teacher's teaching, and of Sawaki's teaching as well. Isn't that what I really did come for?

Jōkō continued, "The body becomes the 'body *as it is*' . . . . The body is the universe, isn't it?"

"What a beautiful leap," I thought.

Jōkō resumed, "Breathing is the work of the universe; it's not the work of your individual self. Thinking, too, is the work of the universe. And as is written in the

Genjōkoan, delusion and realization are one—both a part of the same scenery. So bringing your body back to the universe is zazen (the essence of zazen). Hence, Sawaki Roshi's statement 'By yourself you make the self your self.' Truly, you become your self. And that *is* the universe. That *this thing* becomes *this thing* is the form of the universe. If you want to become something else, you are making a mistake. You need to be satisfied with who you are."

Jōkō quoted Sawaki and Dōgen far more than his own teacher. Later he told me that Sawaki described the teaching from many angles so that all could understand it. "My teacher," he said, "didn't have the ability to do that. But," he added, "my teacher sifted the essence from Sawaki Roshi's teachings better than anyone else could."

Jōkō called his house Kōkazan Senriji, after a saying that is the subject of many of Yokoyama's calligraphies—*kōka senri,* meaning "fragrant mist travels a thousand leagues." Zen temples usually have two names, a mountain name, often ending in *san* or *zan*—hence Kōkazan or Fragrant Mist Mountain—and temple name ending in *dera* or *ji*—hence Senriji, or Thousand League Temple. Only its name and its inhabitant qualified it as a temple. The building was very ordinary, like any country house in that region of Japan. And the monk too was quite ordinary, at least in appearance. Of course, in spite of appearances both temple and monk were utterly unique.

He invited me to spend the night and I did.

We sat together that evening and the next morning and I said goodbye. I had been so caught up in the simple life and teaching of Jōkō that I left with many unasked questions about Yokoyama. Jōkō invited me to come again and I assured him that I would. He walked me to the bus stop. Though my work there was still incomplete, it was the end of a wonderful visit.

I left Jōkō's house-temple excited and confused. Yokoyama sat in the park entertaining travelers, as he called them, with his music and hoping to influence them to do zazen. He said that he moved to Komoro and sat in the park near a monument inscribed with a poem by the Japanese poet Tōson Shimazaki because many travelers passed by. Some of them, he believed, would embrace the practice. He felt he could transmit the practice only if he practiced it. Everyone, he once wrote, had some interest in zazen and seeing him practice would arouse that interest in others. He was "offering his body to zazen."

There may have been others who were encouraged to practice after seeing this strange monk in the park sitting in zazen, though I knew of none. But Yokoyama did find someone to follow his example: the person whose house I had just left. Ironically, however, Jōkō did not join him as a result of meeting him in the park, but rather after meeting him at Antaiji, the temple Yokoyama left in order to follow his quest. And now this follower was sitting in his house with an unlisted phone number and nobody sitting with him. I asked Jōkō how he planned to let people know that he had a zendō.

"I don't know," he said. "I really have no idea." He then looked at me and said, "How did you make the connection? I had no notion of you showing up, yet here you are."

I decided to publish excerpts from our conversation in a magazine for which I sometimes wrote articles. I corresponded with Jōkō through the next two years. I had hoped to return sooner but circumstances kept me from visiting Japan for a few years. When I did visit Jōkō last summer he was still sitting alone. This did not seem to bother him one bit. He was like Bodhidharma waiting patiently for the second patriarch to show up, waiting by facing the wall.

My second visit with Jōkō was different. After my last visit and many letters, I regarded us as friends. Almost three years had gone by, and I had undergone many changes, in my own estimation. If Jōkō had experienced any major changes in his life, it wasn't apparent. He hadn't aged much, he wore the same monk's work clothes, and he was as animated as ever. There was no formality or hesitancy between us. He led me into the dining area for tea.

I was happy to be with him again and had to remind myself to stay on target this time. Two things were on my mind. I wanted to find out more about Yokoyama's last days and I wanted to hear Jōkō's thoughts on some statements Sawaki had made during the war years; statements that had recently become controversial in America. *Zen at War*, a book by Brian Victoria, had been published, and it accused Sawaki, among others, of promoting war and using Zen to support Japan's aggression in Asia.

I showed Jōkō some of Sawaki's statements made during World War II with the hope of getting him to talk about their contrariness to Buddha Dharma, but I didn't get very far. The discussion quickly moved to the relative world of human values versus the absolute world of zazen, following precisely the argument that Victoria indicted as the method employed by some Buddhist priests to justify morally reprehensible behavior.

Jōkō didn't see flaws in Sawaki's reasoning, only different ways of interpreting his statements. I wasn't comfortable with what I was trying to do in the first place, sneaking this unexpected topic into our conversation, so I dropped it. My real concern was to know more about Yokoyama's and Sawaki's ideas about zazen. Jōkō was open to talking about anything, but he wasn't expecting me to bring up questions about politics. He would need time to digest this question about Sawaki and the war. I suspect he had never thought about it.

I was beginning to realize that zazen was not a cure-all. People who attain a certain degree of understanding of zazen begin to understand zazen, period. I had to remind myself not to expect Jōkō to be equipped to advise me how to live my life or to decide important ethical questions such as the proper stance of religion toward war. He could tell me about his teacher and about zazen—two things he devoted his life to. I tried to keep focused on those two areas. I was reminded again of Uchiyama talking of his dream that after practicing zazen he would become brave like his teacher. "After thirty years" he said, "I'm still the same old wimp."

"People will never be pure," Jōkō said, "They do zazen letting go of their discriminating mind. Sawaki criticized the belief that people can be egoless," he added. "But they can believe in the purity of the universe—expressed in zazen." Now he was using Yokoyama's expression, which brought me to my main objective. I wanted to know if Yokoyama in his later years talked about his impending death.

"He didn't talk about his impending death as far as I can recall," Jōkō said, "but I do remember an interesting incident."

He proceeded to tell me a story of a fellow who came to visit his teacher two days before Yokoyama's death.

"This fellow came from Tokyo to see my teacher. First he went to the park, hoping to see him there. When he realized my teacher wasn't in the park, he came to the boarding house. He wanted to talk with him.

"He asked me if he could talk with Roshi. Remember, this was two days before Roshi's death. He couldn't stand or even sit up. I didn't know how to respond. This guy had come all the way from Tokyo. On the other hand, my teacher was dying. I didn't feel I could make a decision by myself so I went to the second floor where my teacher was in bed. I told him that this fellow had come from Tokyo to see him, and I asked if he felt up to a meeting. He said he did: 'Ask him to please come up here.'

"I told the visitor that my teacher would see him and I brought him to Roshi's room. Now this fellow started to talk about all his problems. So I'm standing there listening to this fellow who is facing someone on his deathbed and telling him all these personal problems. And I'm wondering how someone can face a dying man and spill out all this personal stuff.

"My teacher remained silent and listened. This is a man who knows he is dying. He just lies there quietly listening to this fellow. Then when the fellow finished talking, my teacher said, 'I am in this condition, dying, and what I say to you I can say with confidence. I am at peace. My mind is at ease. That's why I am clear about what I have to say.'

"He proceeded to write: 'All phenomena are beautiful' (banshō wa uruwashi). He didn't write his usual, 'Red sunset of my home town' (furusatō no yūyake) but rather, 'all phenomena are beautiful.' He couldn't even hold the paper; I had to hold it for him. He was telling this fellow that there aren't any bad things. Not from the point of view of the Buddha. He was saying: 'You are telling me all your problems, but they are only problems from your personal view, because your mind is in that state. If you could free your mind from that state, you would be able to accept everything.'

"It left quite an impression on me."

If I were a good reporter, I might have asked for more. But the story said so much to me that I didn't want to spoil it by pushing further. We drank tea, talked a bit more, and then Jōkō walked me to the bus stop once more. A small group of Indonesian workers who lived in a worker's dormitory near Jōkō's house were waiting for the bus with us. Jōkō asked them how work was going. They struggled with the language but seemed to take delight in the contact. I enjoyed the interaction, particularly because I got a chance to see Jōkō in this new situation.

When I returned to the United States and started to write about my last meeting with Jōkō, I realized that I still wanted to know more. I wrote him asking if he could tell me anything else he could remember of his teacher's final days, weeks, or months.

Jōkō's letter arrived two months later. He had gone through his notes written during Yokoyama's last days and summarized them for me.

O

> Roshi said: It has become quite difficult to make the trip to Kaikoen park. I go thinking, "Just today, just today." I don't want to die outside of the Buddha Way. Without this self [ego], nothing is too difficult to accomplish." (Jōkō's comment: "After this he couldn't walk to the park. He had to use the bus. December through March hardly anyone came to Kaikoen.")

> Roshi said: "The ardor to die a Buddha is more important than living life as a human being."

> Roshi said: "The Buddha Way is following the law of the universe. Never disrupt the order of the universe. I go to Kaikoen so as not to disrupt this order."

> Roshi said: "Being a monk is for the sake of zazen, for no other reason. One has to be ready to bear all hardships, even death, to preserve zazen."

Roshi said (six days prior to Roshi's death): "When people lose their appetite and passion, it is their end. Delusion is power. When delusions disappear power disappears. Sawaki Roshi taught that passion and appetite are offerings to zazen."

Roshi said (three days prior to Roshi's death): "I am grateful to have been able to study Buddhism. I am grateful to have been able to obtain great peace. I was saved by the sunset."[2]

Three poems:

> *The sunset*
> *Unaware of the sunset*
> *Is still the sunset*
>
> *The sunset*
> *Being like this*
> *All phenomena are one sunset*
>
> *The sunset of one's home*
> *Is beautiful*
> *Beautiful like the universe*

Roshi said: "If people come to visit me (after I die), tell them I said thank you."

Roshi said: "Someone asked Sawaki Roshi, 'Is it true that practicing Zen will take away one's fear of death?' Sawaki responded, 'No way. If you practice zazen, your fear of death will increase.'"

Yokoyama's comment: "It is important to be a 'deathless' person. You must know eternal life. Dying and living eternally—ordinary me dies and the Buddha is born. A person dying while alive is the birth of the Buddha. That's the meaning of 'this world is the Pure Land.' Sawaki Roshi said, 'Zazen is dying.' That means zazen is a way that is one with the universe. Zazen is a way to live within the universe and eternity. Death comes no matter what. You must make the universe yourself immediately."

---

[2] One of Yokoyama's early conversion experiences took place while watching the sunset, and the sunset became the subject of many of his poems.

IKEBE'S FINAL YEARS

I last saw Ikebe in the mid 1980s, not long after she had a minor stroke. She still carried herself straight, maintaining her dignity, but her responses were not too clear. She seemed to be somewhere else.

When she told Hiroko and I during our visit in 1976 that she was "given" thirteen more years to live, tears of gratitude were in her eyes. But her last few years may not have been as joyful as they seemed to her then. According to a chronological history compiled by one of her disciples, her last Dharma talk was given January 3, 1984, five years before her death. I can't imagine her giving up Dharma talks unless her physical condition, including her ability to think clearly, had made it impossible. Those must have been difficult years as she was deprived of the activity that she appeared to love most.

Though I'd often returned to Japan after 1984, something prevented me from contacting Ikebe. I knew that if I did go to visit her, I would be seeing a woman who was losing her clarity and her coherence. I suspect I felt a mixture of guilt for not inquiring into her health and relief at being able to remember her at her sharpest and most energetic.

In 1997, when I started writing about her, I knew that I could no longer avoid contacting someone who knew her. I called the telephone number I had from fifteen years before expecting to hear a recorded voice telling me that the number was no longer in service.

"Hello, this is Ikebe" a voice said.

For a second, I was in shock. Then I realized that it wasn't Motoko Ikebe's voice, but that of her adopted daughter Shūko. I recovered and we started to talk. She told me that Ikebe died in 1989, over eight years earlier. I quickly calculated and realized that it was thirteen years from the time she had told us that she was given thirteen more years to live. Though I still believed it was coincidence rather than an affirmation of her psychic powers, I felt happy that she lived as long as she had predicted.

Shūko was excited to hear from me, and her excitement helped relieve some of my guilt for my long silence. She invited Hiroko and I to her home for lunch, and I accepted with reservations, for Shūko was in her seventies and had been sick on and off throughout her life. I didn't want to put her to any trouble, but I did want to see her, so I didn't decline her invitation.

Shūko met us at the bus stop at noon the following day and walked with us to her home. She was living in a small, detached house owned by a disciple of Ikebe. It was lent to Shūko and Ikebe after they moved from a house they rented for a short period in Kyoto. After fifty years in the country previous to their move to Kyoto, the noise from the traffic near their Kyoto house was too much for Ikebe. Nakagawa, her close friend and disciple, offered them her small, detached house and Shūko has been living there ever since. This was the same Nakagawa who had driven Hiroko and I together with a group of Antaiji foreigners to Ikebe's home twenty-five years before. When we arrived at the home, Nakagawa was waiting for us. We sat down, made our greetings, and had tea together.

Shūko talked about her life after Ikebe's death. I don't think I ever heard her talk so much in all the times we'd met previously combined. She had taken ordination from Sawaki when Ikebe was alive. After Ikebe's death she took charge of a small Zen temple. The pressure of the position proved too much for her, having been physically weak most of her life, and she took to her bed. She resigned her position as head priest (*jūshoku*) and soon recovered her health.

Her friend and Dharma sister, Nakagawa, contracted throat cancer ten years before. She was fighting the disease through a vegetarian macrobiotic diet and she appeared healthy and strong as ever. This woman who used to try to get her teacher to eat meat to strengthen her would not touch meat now. Ikebe, who told us of her dilemma when Nakagawa would bring her meat, would have enjoyed seeing her disciple now a devoted vegetarian. Nakagawa, in her characteristically quiet way, left after tea was over.

The generosity of these two women brought back memories of our visits to Ikebe. The service and humility that permeated the atmosphere put us on our best behavior—uptight and uncomfortable.

When we ate with Shūko and Ikebe many years before, it was like being at a temple for the first time. We tried not to make any mistakes in etiquette and found it difficult to enjoy our food as a result. In addition, before eating, we'd recite the "the five remembrances to be had by monks at dinner" (*jukiki go kan no ge*). Since Hiroko and I had never learned this invocation, we would sit with our heads down mumbling something in an effort to "sing along."

So here we were, in the heat of summer, having lunch with a wonderful little woman, and having such mixed feelings. Shūko talked and talked nervously, and we sat and listened—legs folded, backs straight, dripping in sweat. I was happy to see her and dying to leave at the same time. I never even asked the question I wish I had asked: what Ikebe's last years were like.

Ikebe had a sister and brother. According to Shūko, Ikebe's mother said to her, "You are not beautiful like your sister nor brilliant like your brother so your only alternative is to develop your character." Shūko said that Ikebe was so strict about manners that she sometimes felt living with her teacher was extremely energy consuming. We listened, still dripping in sweat and knees aching.

When we had finished, Nakagawa was back doing the dishes. She seemed to thrive on being of service. She talked little but she was very much present. As her teacher had said, "Your actions alone will be a great sermon. Sermonizing is not the real teaching. It is theater." Nakagawa did talk about how devoted Shūko was to her teacher in Ikebe's final year. Ikebe was confined to bed and could not do anything for herself, and Shūko was there for her. Shūko walked us to the bus stop and we said our goodbyes.

Shūko respected her teacher greatly. Ikebe was her guide and may even have saved her from a nervous breakdown. Rejecting her own family of conservative rice farmers who, wanting her to marry and live a "normal" life, could never understand her desire to become a nun, she became Ikebe's adopted daughter. Ikebe treated her like a disciple and like a daughter. In this double role, Ikebe was doubly strict. Shūko said it was difficult living with someone as strict as Ikebe, but she said it in a way that made you feel she had no regrets for the choice she made. Shūko talked about Ikebe in very human terms and with much love. When she talked about her teacher, I felt I was getting closer to a real person—Ikebe was becoming dearer to me.

Shūko was getting old and was suffering from hearing loss. Writing was becoming difficult for her and telephone conversations were near impossible. I decided to e-mail another disciple who has continued attending the zazen meetings and who helped publish Ikebe's talks after her death. I asked him if he could tell me what he remembered about his teacher's final years. He e-mailed me a summary of his journal during that period, which, in addition to giving information about Ikebe's final years, reveals the attitude of one of Ikebe's disciples toward his teacher.

The following account of Ikebe's last years is translated from Munehiko Maeda's journal.

○

> March 22, 1986. Sensei was hospitalized with a stroke. She is eighty-eight years old. The sorrow of an old body! It is the fate of everyone. Sensei doesn't have long to live. I feel so sad for Shūko, her adopted daughter. We have to be prepared. I want to visit her as much as possible.

> January 19, 1987. Sensei is bedridden, but she appears to be in better spirits than before. She once said to me, "Maeda-san, each person has his own fate. You are already sixty-seven and you haven't attained the Way. If you realize unconditional love in your heart, your fate can change.

You must open your eyes."
I am grateful for these words.

April 19, 1987. Sensei moved to a home for the aged, "Green Mountain Home," in Nose. I feel sad seeing her lying in her bed—she seems like a symbol of the aged dying. However, when she noticed me she smiled and held my hand tightly. I remember she once said, "When I have nothing to give to people, I want to at least offer them a smile." I regretted having done nothing for her up to now. She had wanted to go to a place with a warm climate but I didn't take her—how regrettable!

November 11, 1988. At Sensei's home. She's hooked up to an ISV. Together with friends I practice zazen near her.

June 26, 1989. I watch Sensei as she has difficulty breathing, bedridden. How few will be the chances to see her!

July 31, 1989. Sensei is on her deathbed. This may be the end. Just as I had these thoughts, Sensei opened her eyes and gazed at us. She is watching over us. She realizes that death is near.

October 17, 1989. I visited Sensei. She noticed me. When I placed my hand on her forehead, it seemed to make her feel more comfortable. I thought, with death before her eyes she tastes the peace of mind from meditation while in bed. My teacher!

October 27, 1989. Sensei died at 6:50 PM. Ah, life is fleeting! Could anything touch my soul more deeply than Sensei's death? I vow to myself: I will follow her teaching. In this short life, I will live in the here and now, throw away everything, become a skeleton with only this thought. I will make an effort to live this vow and someday the true life will shine.

○

Until reading Maeda's description of Ikebe's final years, I hadn't realized how difficult it must have been for those so close to her and so dependent on her guidance to watch her leave this world in the way she did, bedridden and drifting in and out of consciousness for over a year while they could do little for her. For years, they had been listening to her tell them of the impermanence of the relative world and of the importance of placing their faith in the world of the absolute. They must have tried to understand and accept what she said, but to watch her linger on for years and finally in the last few months in a state of semi-consciousness—the real sermon for them—was not as easy to accept.

Ikebe left the world in her ninetieth year. The disciples only had each other, her memory, and the practice of zazen. They bemoaned losing her, wrote about their loss, some even using such epitaphs as "the Virgin Mother" and "the Bodhisattva Avalokiteshvara" in their descriptions of her. Ikebe was a giant in the eyes of her disciples, and her death left a vacuum in their lives. But her talks always stressed the need for zazen and she had them practice zazen as the core of each of their meetings, at which she also gave Dharma talks. When she became too weak to sit with them, she still lectured and they continued sesshins.

After Ikebe's stroke, she could no longer give talks. Her disciples still visited her and continued their regular sesshins, usually arranged by Mizuno, a devoted longstanding disciple. It is over ten years since her death and the group continues to hold sesshins and listens to audiotapes of Ikebe's talks. They are reminded through these tapes to be present and to see zazen as the most important means of bringing the present into their lives.

Mizuno transcribes her talks, which comprise a major part of a monthly newsletter he publishes called *Nyōze*. Together with Maeda he has completed four books containing Ikebe's talks and short tributes to her by friends and students. The following passages are from volume 4 of *Ikiru Shisei o Motomete*.

> You won't attain a settled mind [quiet mind] unless you practice zazen. That's why they [teachers] are always saying "Zazen, zazen." Though you do zazen, it will bring you nothing.[3] That means that even though you practice zazen you really won't get anything—you won't become smarter, you won't get richer. In fact you might lose something. Still as you sit more and more, you will come to a point where you can't bear not sitting. Then, as you become comfortable [with yourself], your mind will quiet down and you will feel settled.
>
> When you truly practice zazen, you are not performing a ceremony in which you sit and pile up merit—reciting ten thousand *nembutsu* [praise to Amida Buddha] or vowing to chant the phrase for one year—and then

---

[3] Probably taken from Kōdō Sawaki's constant refrain.

receive some benefit from it. You just sit. You sit so that your clear mind will always *be here*, quietly and purely. You sit so that the shadow of the three poisons will creep away. So sit as much as you can . . . because you can sit.

The human world is the world of time and the world of place—of time and space. You must always take one step at a time. You must never give up, you must move on unflaggingly. Though you think that if you keep walking you will finally arrive at your goal, it doesn't work that way. [You have to practice so that] If you were to suddenly fall over [and die], you will have given your all. You always have to give your all. Every instant must be everything to you. The whole universe is embodied in it now—that is the posture you must have.

This instant, giving your whole body and soul, you drop the world of the three poisons.[4] That's all we humans can do. Continue in this way and your mind will quiet down, you will become clearer and feel easier. You will definitely recognize when you are at ease.

So always empty your heart in the reality of zazen—an hour of zazen is said to be an hour of the Tathagata [Buddha]. Keeping the Tathagata in your mind, staying here, not allowing delusion to flourish, that alone is religious practice. . . . Tathagata is already here, causing us to breathe, operating the five sensory organs. The Tathagata is the main image that gives life to the senses. It is right here, but is covered with a veil of delusion, so we don't know it.

You just have to remove the delusion, that's all. Religious practice is simply ceasing to create delusion. When you cease creating delusion, the truth alone remains. Then the true-life function will manifest from inside of you. That is love; love and compassion are the true-life function. Mean thoughts are delusion, aren't they? They will cease appearing completely. Love will always reveal itself. What you want to do for others, what you need to do for others, will be at your disposal. The understanding of how to work for others—love and wisdom—will make themselves known.

The Buddhist scriptures talk of compassion and wisdom. The bible speaks of love and wisdom. They will actually come to light. It is truly a wonder. Just from ceasing to create delusion. Just exerting all your effort for that. That's all you have to do. Always letting go from your heart. That's all religious practice is.

---

[4] Covetousness, anger, and delusion.

Shūko, who had lived with Ikebe for over thirty years and nursed her through her last years, describes her final days eloquently in the first volume of *Ikiru Shisei o Motomete:*

> Though in Ikebe's last three years she suffered outwardly from a stroke, I'm brimful of warm memories of her [inner] vitality and how she exhausted her energy making sure there was a plan in place for me to live on my own.
>
> As death approached, she refrained from eating, to clean out her body. I believe that she was discarding attachments through the actions of a strong will.
>
> For eight days she drank only dark brown rice tea and her stomach was completely emptied out. It was as though the skin covering her stomach was flat against the skin of her back.
>
> When Mizuno said to her, "Put your mind at rest, we will hold strong," she nodded deeply and instantly tears flowed. Then her breathing stopped.
>
> Eternal separation. I touched her cheek; it was cold like a stone. When I realized that our relationship in this world was severed, an inexpressible sadness filled my heart.

BACK TO ANTAIJI AND UCHIYAMA

The trip to Hamasaka through the mountains of Northern Hyōgo Prefecture was breathtaking. My daughter, Nao, who was staying with her grandparents in Sakai City, had wanted to see the real backcountry in Japan. I wished I had taken her. I was visiting the new Antaiji and it was in the middle of a practice period so I didn't think it would be right to take her. Now I was regretting my decision.

I hadn't seen the new Antaiji since the construction was completed. I visited once before I moved to the States. The buildings were under construction then while the monks were living in the one temporary building. They were the construction crew.

My mind started to wander as I watched the towns disappear and the lush green of rice paddies and mountains of cedars, camphor, pines, and oaks dominate the view. I remember my surprise when I received a letter from Tesshō with the return address, "Antaiji, Hamasaka."

I visited him at his apartment in Kumagaya City. I went there on the chance that I would find him, though he hadn't answered my letters and never answered the phone. I knocked on his door and was surprised that he was there.

"Arthur, it's been a long time. Come on in." He put up tea.

"I called and wrote you, but got no reply. I came to see whether you were alive."

"I'm sorry. I keep the phone's ring on low so I can do zazen."

"You didn't answer my postcards either," I pressed relentlessly.

"My salary from my new job is quite low. I have no money for stamps," he said laughing. "I don't even have money for beer. I have to drink cheap *shōchū*."

"Let me treat you this time, then." I went to the grocery and bought a six pack and some snacks. When I got back he was washing dishes. I poured some beer. "I was quite surprised when I received your letter from Hamasaka. What brought you to Antaiji?"

"I heard they had built a temple from scratch and were trying to live exclusively off what they produced. It sounded like an exciting place to practice, so I tried it."

"Why did you leave?"

"I came there to practice, but Watanabe Roshi wanted me to teach. I was the only monk that had a background in Buddhist texts. It wasn't what I expected, so I left."

"I met Zuihō from Antaiji when the monks were helping out for the Obon festival in Kyoto a few years back." (Obon, the festival for the dead, is a Buddhist holiday.) "He said that all you talked about was Krishnamurti. And that you said temple life was bullshit."

"Did I say that?" he said, laughing.

"I thought it was pretty funny because now I'm teaching at a Krishnamuti school and trying to practice Zen, and here you are a Zen monk preaching Krishnamurti. Are you through with Zen?"

"I have no desire to become a layman, if that's what you mean. I have no regrets about being a monk. I just learned a little more about the meaning of monkhood from Krishnamurti. But I learned more about *shūgyō* (religious practice) from my last two jobs."

"What kind of work were you doing?"

"I worked in a hardware store. It was really tough. Here I am, this fifty-year-old guy taking orders from all these customers, searching for bolts, nuts, screws, sheets of iron, rolls of mesh, this size and that size; getting it wrong and having to go back and find things quickly because everyone is in a rush—it was real *shūgyō*, I'm not kidding."

"And now?" I asked.

"Now I'm really doing backbreaking work. But I prefer it to office work. I tried that once. I work in a bottling plant. I have to carry heavy equipment. It keeps me in shape. I've burnt myself a few times, but I'm still alive."

"Do you ever think of going back to a temple?"

"I have many friends in temples. They try to get me to go back. But I don't think I could do that anymore," he said laughing.

The following day we went to my friend Owen's house in Tokyo and I put on a Krishnamurti videotape for Tesshō. He watched for over an hour, eyes glued to the screen. I was sure he couldn't understand much of the English but that didn't bother him at all. He was totally absorbed in the visuals. When the tape was over I took him to the train station. I watched him as he walked off and I wondered what he would be doing the next time we met. Goodbye Ikkyū-san.

O

As the train emerged from a short tunnel the beauty of the lush mountains woke me from my daydreams. I must ask Shinyū, the present abbot, if I can bring Nao here as soon as the training period ends.

"Shinyū, the present abbot"—how quickly time's passed. He was a young man who appeared at the old Antaiji in 1976 just after Uchiyama had retired. Kōhō Watanabe was the new abbot then, and together with the resident monks he was busy tearing down the old temple. The Kyoto Antaiji, once a small monastery in the middle of a large field, by 1976 was closed in by private homes, apartment houses, and a college dormitory. Construction was constantly going on in the area, and the *Hooo... huuu... hooo... huuu...* from the horn of the tofu man, the song of the sweet potato vendor, and loudspeakers announcing the candidates to the next election all sounded against the static *da-da-da-da-dat* of air hammers. Watanabe, who loved large-scale projects and couldn't endure the ever-increasing sound pollution of Antaiji's neighborhood, sold the land during that period and bought property in the countryside in the hope of regaining some tranquility in rural Japan. Soaring property values in Kyoto allowed him to buy an entire abandoned village by the Sea of Japan near the city of Tottori for the money received from selling the small parcel of land that was Antaiji.

"I knew nothing of Zen, nor did I know that people still did zazen. I was working for a company and I had had enough of that world. I wanted to become a monk, which to me meant dropping out of the world," Shinyū later told me.

Watanabe must have realized that this novice needed a dose of zazen to wake him up. There was no zazen happening at the half-demolished Antaiji just then, so the abbot told him to sit with the foreigners—a group of us were holding our own sesshins at George's house. George was a British guy who lived in an old country house in Himuro, a small village outside of Kyoto. While Antaiji was being torn down we decided to use George's house for sesshins because it was fairly spacious and quiet. Shinyū joined us and we had to show him how to sit. The role reversal was kind of fun—for us at least. Shinyū followed our instructions and quietly bore the pain, but he didn't seem to be enjoying it any better than we had when we started years ago.

When I called Shinyū from Osaka twenty-five years later, I wondered whether he would remember me. He did, and said that they were in the middle of sesshin but that I should come anyway. I took the train to Hamasaka the next day. Hamasaka, a fishing village on the coast of the Sea of Japan, is the closest town to Antaiji with a train station. Antaiji is sixteen kilometers southeast of Hamasaka.

From Hamasaka I took a bus to Ikeganaruguchi, a bus stop at the foot of a mountain called Ikeganaru. Antaiji is located four kilometers up a winding road that starts near the bus stop. Three old women rode the bus with me from Hamasaka. With each stop more old people boarded the bus and they all seemed to know each other. I listened carefully to the conversations but the country dialect eluded me—except for some simple greetings and small talk. What I could decipher made me feel good.

"Ueda couldn't make it today?" one woman asked an old man boarding the bus.

"Yeah, she caught a cold and had to stay home."

I wondered where they were going, but felt too shy to ask. Then the bus intercom announced, "Next stop is Hamasaka Hospital."

Suddenly all the old people got off the bus talking in animated fashion as though they were going on a picnic. Their outing was their regular visit to the local hospital for their free checkup, blood-pressure tests, and medicine. And poor Ueda couldn't make it because she was sick.

Many villages like Hamasaka were becoming old-age homes, as most of the young people moved to the big cities to get better jobs, leaving their parents and grandparents behind. There was some tourist traffic, as there were hot springs in the area, but jobs were not plentiful and opportunities for advancement were practically nil. The new Antaiji was built in an old, abandoned village which even the elderly found too remote and the weather too severe.

I had called Antaiji from Hamasaka Station, so when I got off the bus a German monk, Muhō, was waiting for me. Muhō was cook (*tenzo*) for the sesshin and was dressed in work clothes that made him resemble Charlie Chaplin. The fly zipper from his pants was broken and he seemed not in the least concerned. I wondered whether he enjoyed the cool breeze it provided.

Muhō took off in a small pickup truck with me by his side. He drove the old truck up the steep hills and sharp turns like a cowboy. My attention was drawn to the beauty of the surrounding hills and the sounds of the birds, only to be brought back to my primary concern, my life, as Muhō flew around another sharp turn. He had obviously made the trip often and knew the roads well, but the sharp drop at the side of the road on those turns frightened me so much that I was in no condition to admire his skill.

Shinyū came to greet me at the entrance and led me to his room. Muhō disappeared. I feared Shinyū might lead me straight to the zendō to get me back for the pain in his legs twenty-five years before at George's in Himuro, but he didn't. We talked through most of the afternoon sittings. With two sesshins a month, one for five days at the beginning of the month and another for three days in the middle of the month, Shinyū must have welcomed the relief.

There were no pretenses about him. I was talking with a friend; we were reminiscing about old times while learning about each other. I had to remind myself that he was abbot of Antaiji, the fourth generation in the Sawaki-Uchiyama line.

He told me about his life before entering Antaiji. He worked for a Japanese company as his father did before him. His father had worked all his life, looking forward to retiring and enjoying his free time, but no sooner did he retire than he died. Shinyū couldn't forget that, and it made him question his own life and its meaning. Was he destined to share the same fate? He had saved some money from his years in the company so he quit and spent a year traveling around the world. His plan was to become a monk when he returned to Japan. A friend told him about Zen Buddhism and suggested he enter a Zen temple, recommending two temples: Antaiji and Ryūtakuji. Ryūtakuji might be too severe, the friend said, so Shinyū chose Antaiji. When he heard that the main practice at Antaiji was sitting, he envisioned monks sitting around a table talking over tea. I now had a better idea of what must have been going through his mind when he joined us for his first sesshin at Himuro.

Shinyū took me around the grounds while we continued our talk. There were only five monks including Shinyū there at that time—just enough to handle the work of a property of that size and in that condition. In fact, Shinyū said that he thought ten monks were required to properly run the temple; they had more than twenty at times, but that was too many. I asked why, and he replied that they would start forming cliques and factions then. I wondered how the temples of old managed with more than a thousand monks in residence.

The new Antaiji is on a mountain surrounded by higher peaks. Blue hydrangea dot the landscape, the result of one plant brought from the old Antaiji in 1976.

How different this huge property was from the small Kyoto Antaiji! The isolation from civilization one felt there was remarkable. The only sounds were the birds, the cicadas, and the wind in the trees. With the exception of the cherry trees in spring and the hydrangea in summer, it was a vast expanse of different shades of green. How rare to find only one building on one hundred and twenty-five acres of land in this crowded country! The experience of being in these mountains after a week in Osaka was exhilarating for both its sheer physical beauty and the mystical atmosphere of the place. While marveling at the view, I was reminded of the fact that I was an outsider. As one of the resident monks later said to me when I remarked about the beauty that surrounded him, "Where you see beauty we see fields that need to be taken care of and weeds that need to be pulled."

Shinyū then led me to a place in back of the temple where there were little pagodas in memory of monks who lived at or had some important connection with Antaiji, leading me from a world of natural beauty and awareness of the present to a world of memory. Here before me were stones telling the history of the old Antaiji and thus the origin of the temple on whose grounds I was standing. Some meant little to me personally—such as the first stone Shinyū pointed to, for Sōtan Oka, a famous Dōgen scholar and Sōtō priest in whose name the old Antaiji was founded in 1921. Kōdō Sawaki, who had studied for a period under Oka Roshi, was next. I knew more of Kōdō Sawaki and he meant more to me than Oka, but I looked at it without much emotion.

"That one is for a monk named Shōgen," Shinyū said, pointing to another stone. This jolted my memory, for I remembered Shōgen well. He was one of the monks at Antaiji when I moved in there in the summer of 1969, an emotionally fragile man who eventually committed suicide. I wondered how much of his story Shunyū knew, but I said nothing.

Each pagoda brought with it another memory.

"That one is for Jōshin-san," Shinyū said.

At my last meeting with Shūkō, Ikebe's adopted daughter, she talked about Jōshin.

"It was very sad at the end," Shūkō said about her friend. "She would take off and nobody knew where she was. People would be out searching for her."

Jōshin, so independent all her life, probably tried to hold on to her independence when she was no longer capable of taking care of herself. She tried to continue her wandering ways, but she would get lost.

Jōshin and Shūkō's friendship went far back, as it was Jōshin who encouraged Shūkō to take ordination from Sawaki. "It may be the last chance to be ordained by Roshi," Jōshin had told her. "His health is failing and he won't be around long." Shūkō followed her friend's advice and was ordained by Sawaki at his final ordination ceremony, which was in the early 1960s. How difficult it must have been for Shūkō to see this woman whom she looked up to as a big sister, this little powerhouse of a human being who followed her heart and overcame whatever obstacles were in her way, lose control of her own faculties.

I remembered visiting Jōshin in her little cabin at old Antaiji just before I left Japan. She was making a meditation cushion for me. She invited me to have some tea with her. After pouring me some black tea, she went to her closet and took out a fifth of Johnny Walker and poured some in both of our cups. Aha! I thought to myself, so that's how this little lady kept her spirits up!

I started to talk to Shinyū about Jōshin.

"I'd heard that one of the first things on the agenda when you all moved up here from old Antaiji was to build a place for Jōshin."

"Yes it was."

"It must have been difficult for her to live in this harsh country."

"Yes, it gets very cold and the snow piles quite high during the winter months. I actually had to carry her down from here on my back in November of 1983. Sure enough, the first snow came the next day. That was her last day here. She died in May of the following year. She was seventy then."

The next pagoda was Uchiyama's: the founder, in name, of the new Antaiji; the abbot of the old Antaiji until his retirement; and the man who taught me zazen for five years, and about whom I still had very conflicted feelings after all these years.

O

I had visited Japan at least five times from the late 1980s to mid-1990s and always managed to avoid visiting Uchiyama—I realize now because I was trying to avoid any disappointment that might be caused by the gap between my image of him and the reality, in both past and present. In the winter of 1996 I wrote to Tom, a friend of mine and a disciple of Uchiyama, expressing my hope that I could visit my teacher one more time and talk about my feelings about practicing with him. Tom wrote back that Roshi was dying and probably wouldn't regain consciousness, but that spring Uchiyama miraculously recovered.

I was visiting Japan the following summer and made plans to visit him when Tom and Dōyū, another disciple, were scheduled to visit. Some business got in the way and I couldn't make it that day. I wondered whether I would end up avoiding a meeting again. But I was writing this story about my years at Antaiji when Uchiyama was abbot and I knew it was imperative to see him; more than that, however, I simply wanted to thank him for this special practice he had taught me.

One day, when I was returning to my in-laws home in Sakai City, I found myself about an hour away from Shiojiri, a small town where Uchiyama spent his summers to escape the heat of Kyoto. I picked up a public phone and called. His wife Keiko answered.

"Hello"

"Hello, this is Arthur. I studied at Antaiji when Roshi was there. We've met several times since Roshi's retirement."

"Yes, I remember you. How are you?"

"Fine, thank you. I called to make an appointment to see Roshi. It's already late, so another day would be fine."

"Where are you?"

"I'm at Nagano Station."

"That's less than an hour from here. It's only four o'clock. Please come now. Roshi has spent the day in bed. When visitors come it gives him energy."

"OK, I'll come right over."

Keiko gave me directions and with feelings of excitement and anxiety I started on my way to their house. I don't really know why I was anxious, since Uchiyama has always been a warm host and a lively conversationalist. It must have been the old ambivalence of my feelings and the ensuing guilt that made me apprehensive, but the excitement of seeing an old teacher and friend prevailed as I made my way to his house. Shiojiri, like so many Japanese towns, was dense with houses and stores that looked alike, and I got lost twice. I finally made it to his house with the help of a friendly citizen of the town. Keiko met me at the door and led me to a room adjacent to a verandah facing a small Japanese garden with a pond, pine trees, patches of moss, and some shrubs. We were shaded from the sun and a cool, late afternoon breeze made the spot quite pleasant. Uchiyama was just getting out of bed and Keiko brought me a cool drink and asked me to make myself comfortable while I waited. I gave her some cakes I had picked up at Shiojiri Station and sat down and enjoyed the breeze and the view.

Uchiyama was now eighty-five years old; he'd had failing health for the twenty-eight years I had known him and was a frail man all his life. I hadn't seen him in over seven years. When he joined us, I was shocked at how much he had aged. I had visited Jōkō, a former disciple of Uchiyama, a week before my visit to Shiojiri, and he warned me that Uchiyama had aged, but I was still surprised. Most of his teeth were gone, he had a special hearing device that he carried in his pocket, and walking was difficult for him. But when he began to talk, a youthfulness I remembered well took over.

"It's been a long time, Arthur. How are you?"

"Yes it has. I'm fine. How have you been?"

"I'm okay now. I died once but I've come back," he said with a laugh, and went on to describe a period of about a month the previous autumn when he lay in bed barely conscious.

I wanted to ask him about old Antaiji, his relationship with Yokoyama and Ikebe, and get more information for my story, but it became clear pretty soon that he wasn't interested in discussing that. He had no desire to talk about old friends or bygone days.

"Roshi, when we were training at Antaiji. . . ."

"I'm not interested in the past," he cut me off. "I'm interested in the future, which for me means death. I could die at any moment. I did die once," he repeated. "The fact that I could die at any moment interests me greatly."

"I remember the first talk I ever heard you give. It was in 1970. What stood out in my mind then was what you said about death. You said you might die tomorrow or you might live many years, but it was all the same." I wasn't consciously attempting to bring him back to that period, but if I had I would have been unsuccessful anyway.

"I've spent my life talking about death," he said and continued, "But never with the understanding and immediacy I feel now." There was no futility in what he said or in the way he said it. It was truly the wonder of a new awareness and a new nearness to death.

"Since life and death are one and the same, my life is rich for my understanding of death."

He paused for a moment and then continued. "The zazen I did most of my life has prepared me for old age. Old age is constant zazen. Most people have difficulty with old age because they are experiencing it for the first time. They haven't experienced it in youth, as I have through zazen."

He repeated over and over that zazen and old age were the same.

"I wish my father had your spirit with regard to death," I said.

"Let me get you something I wrote recently about dying. Please give it to your father."

Keiko brought a paper with Uchiyama's poems on dying and served the cakes. We started to eat. I became concerned whether Uchiyama, with his two remaining teeth, would be able to eat them, but he was chomping away.

"These cakes are very good, Arthur."

"I bought them at the Shiojiri Station. The woman behind the stand said you would like them."

I talked a bit with Keiko about Kyoto, where she grew up, and listened to her lament having had to live away from the old capital in order to be with Uchiyama, and how she missed her friends and family there. It was a bit like talking to someone from ancient Japan, when exile from the capital was regarded as a fate worse than death. Then she went away, either into the kitchen or the garden to do some work. Uchiyama talked about a recent TV appearance he made and how he spent most of the program talking about death.

It was getting dark and I thought I should prepare to say goodbye. A man named Shimizu who, I gather, donated this house to Uchiyama for the hot summer months usually dropped by after work to have a few words. After talking with Mr. Shimizu, Roshi would retire. It was a little routine Uchiyama must have become accustomed to.

"I wonder why Shimizu hasn't come yet?" Uchiyama muttered to himself.

Then a few minutes later he asked, "Keiko, Mr. Shimizu hasn't arrived yet?"

"Not yet."

"He's usually here by now." Uchiyama spoke half to himself and half to me.

I started rehearsing my goodbyes. "You must be tired Roshi, so I'll take my leave." Or "Thank you for taking the time to talk with me. It's getting late and you must be tired." And then I wondered if I should wait a little longer for Mr. Shimizu to show up. But I couldn't say a word.

Uchiyama then turned the conversation to a fellow, one of the first American students, who had recently come to Japan to visit him. This fellow lived in Hawaii. He came every day for almost a month to see Uchiyama and be of help in whatever way he could.

"Arthur, do you know that fellow Fred?"

"I know the name and a little about him. He came to Antaiji a year before I did."

"He visited me recently. He would come every day and give me wonderful massages." Uchiyama stared out into the garden and then, perhaps feeling ready to retire, looked around and said, "Where is Mr. Shimizu? Keiko, Mr. Shimizu hasn't come yet?"

"Not yet."

I thought I'd better thank him and leave, but I still couldn't say anything. Then I mumbled that it was getting late and perhaps I should leave, but I don't think he heard me. The next moment he said, "I guess Mr. Shimizu isn't coming. You had better go now Arthur, I'm getting tired."

The realization that it was time for me to leave was in both our minds but Uchiyama had a much easier time expressing it than I did. Uchiyama and Keiko saw me to the door, thanked me for coming, and asked me to come again. We bowed to each other and I walked quickly to the train station.

On the train back to Osaka I thought about the meeting. I was uncomfortable some of the time, but in no way did Uchiyama make me uncomfortable. He was gracious as ever and still full of life. I came with all kinds of questions and didn't get a chance to ask any of them. My main purpose, I thought, was to thank him for the years of teaching and to let him know that I now, after twenty-eight years, see the true wisdom in his approach to zazen, but the words never came out. What I thought was my primary reason for seeing him wasn't really very important. *But seeing him was.* He was very human and he did not want us to see him any other way. I remembered his words about Sawaki's charisma being an obstacle and wondered how many times I would have to hear them before they would actually sink in.

Uchiyama had the most profound approach to Buddhism that I ever encountered, but I was so caught up in the matter of his personality that I was missing his Dharma. In a very subtle way he was reminding me of my tendency to let his personality get in the way of his Dharma. His personality was not bad—he was charming, witty, interesting and a good host. But he wasn't perfect, and as long as I probed his personality instead of just listening to his teaching, I would find human imperfections. I was reminded of Uchiyama's remark about his teacher, Sawaki, in an interview about a month before Uchiyama's death. He said, "Sawaki Roshi was not my 'true teacher.' Sawaki Roshi, too, was a deluded person *(bombu)*."

This statement, taken out of context, might make one feel that he was ungrateful to the man he studied under for over twenty-five years. He added however, "I've always told my disciples that the true teacher is inside each one of them and that they should search for him there."

I believe that he saw the danger when we idolize people, as he may have done at some time with his teacher. Perhaps he wanted to prepare his students for the fact that we are all basically alone. And, I might add, we can help each other in our aloneness and that is where we are connected. When Uchiyama faced the wall during sesshin, neither lecturing nor holding private meetings, he was giving us his most profound teaching: *Do zazen, depend on nobody, and I too will join you in this practice.*

On March 14 I received a call from one of Uchiyama's disciples, Dōyū Takamine, saying Uchiyama died peacefully in his sleep the previous day. A week later my friend Michael wrote telling me about the funeral:

> It was the start of the last zazenkai (March 14) that Dōyū informed us of Uchiyama Roshi's death the previous evening. Dōyū and his wife Hideko had gone to Uji and spent the night there.

It seems Roshi had a sense his death was coming and had been making some final preparations during the previous week. The day of his death he had been up and around.

The funeral was Monday, March 16, and the ceremony took place inside his house with about forty people in the room and another forty standing outside.

You would have recognized most of the monks—the twenty-five years since most of them had been together slipped away, and they all seemed like floating clouds, keeping in the background (some even wearing samue), but allowing everything to move along with dignity and great feeling. Kōhō-san never left Uchiyama's Roshi's wife's side.

The brief ceremony ended with a period of zazen and then three bows. Roshi's open casket was brought out to the verandah and everyone formed a line to place a flower on his body and made a final bow.

The "weathermark" identifies this book as a production of Weatherhill, publishers of fine books on Asia and the Pacific. Editorial supervision: Jeffrey Hunter. Book and cover design: David Noble. Production Supervision: Bill Rose. The typefaces used are Scala and Scala Sans.

Shambhala Publications
2129 13th Street
US-CO, 80302
US
https://www.shambhala.com
517-424-0030

The authorized representative in the EU for product safety and compliance is

eucomply OÜ
Pärnu mnt 139b-14
CZ, 11317
EE
https://www.eucompliancepartner.com
hello@eucompliancepartner.com
+372 536 865 02

ISBN: 9780834805316
Release ID: 153046648

www.ingramcontent.com/pod-product-compliance
Lightning Source LLC
Chambersburg PA
CBHW032256150426
43195CB00008BA/475